COPING WITH MADNESS.

A collection of existential 'poetry' and One short story WLTM.

Not for the slavishly politically correct or Over squeamish.

Philip Fletcher

COPING WITH MADNESS is a BLACK SUN e-PRESS PRODUCTION.

Copyright 2008. Philip Fletcher

ISBN 978-09556879-0-7

No part of this work may be reproduced without the author's consent, which he will only give if loads of money's involved; as he's been poor and wretched his whole tortured life.

COPING WITH MADNESS.

I lost what I typed in yesterday, a whole screen full just wiped because I couldn't get to grips with the technology; it could happen again at any time! Anyway, the crux of what I was saying was that C W M should chronologically have been my first or second book (slim vol'), not my third, which is how it's working out. 'VIEWED WITH SUSPICION' 1.3came out last year to rave reviews from me, the man who self published it. I still have a few copies left, well more than a few actually. I'm working on my second slim volume: 'DOWN IN ONE' at Todmorden Community College, putting the work onto floppy disc; I'd say I was about a quarter of the way through with it, and there's only 3 more sessions before the summer term ends. I'd like to have 2 completed titles to take to the Writers Retreat at Lumb Bank in Heptonstall in September, but it's looking rather unlikely right now. Also right now, I'm going to try and save this piece and log off to see if I'll be able to retrieve it, if I can it will be all systems go when I feel like getting round to the back, and eye straining effort, (why do we bother? Why can't we suppress our creative egos? Meaning me of course.)
4/6/02

....

SEEMINGLY NOTHING, BLOKE ON THE DOLE AGED 48   July 1994

Another night's soulless sleep, and one more barren day to come.
I live in a social vacuum; they imply I don't fit in by giving me a wide berth. I sit on my favourite park bench in the early morning light, watching my dog relieving himself in the grass, I must invest in a 'poop scoop' one day; but a vicious streak in me hopes that someone who wouldn't give me the time of day will skid along on it, affording themselves a smelly shock. While he rolls in the dew I work out scenarios for a happy, healthy existence, but they always involve the co-operation of other people, usually females, so they always come to nothing.
An overweight middle-aged woman comes shuffling towards me, led by a squat Scottie dog, my dog suddenly looks alert. She plonks herself down at the other end of the bench, muttering to herself. My dog sniffs her dog's behind, her dog tries to bite his nose off. A yapping and snarling contest ensues, I can't be bothered to call mine off and she seems to be preoccupied. The two canines get tired of each other and go off in different directions; the hopeless case stares straight ahead, telling someone off who only she can see. Even the birds are in a bad mood, scrapping in the trees. The early morning sunshine is taken over by cloud, a few spots of rain, I might as well go home and back to bed for a few hours.

....

# THE UNOBTRUSIVE MESSIAH.
1994(?)

Yes, it's me! I'm conducting the whole show from the comfort and sanctuary of my armchair. For 40 years now, I've realised I was different from other mere mortals, and that simply thinking about something gave me the power to change the destiny of mankind. Every positive act that happens in the world theatre is a result of my thinking about it first; I can trace them all back to me. In fact it's with a great sense of magnanimity that I don't seek more credit for my good works. I've taken a vow of anonymity, which is very noble of me because my personal life sucks. I'm always on my own, no-one's even come close to suspecting that it's me who's saved the human race from its final Armageddon.

At times I feel like shouting it out in the street, "IT'S ME! I'M GOD!" but I know what people are like. They'd just slink past me or else stand around smirking, ungrateful bastards. I'm busy saving everybody's skin and I haven't even got a girl friend out of it! I keep telling the great deity I don't want this job any more, but it doesn't seem to listen, it just carries on working through me. In fact I think this is why women steer clear of me, they sense my other worldliness. I think they feel that they wouldn't be free to behave like tarts in bed with me because of my stern and disapproving aura, but it's this horrible mission to make the world a better place that's done this to me. I just want to be a dog like every one else, especially when it comes to sex. Hmmm! Doin' it 'doggie style', my favourite position every time; tho' I can't remember the last time I did it in any position other than lying flat on my back with my massive penis in my hand.

....
....

TOO LITTLE OF TOO MUCH: A 'NOT HAVEALOT' PRODUCTION. 94/95.

"Have you done any work in the last fortnight?"
"Have you got any savings you haven't told us about?"
"Remember, to give false information could lead to prosecution."
"Have you got a TV licence? If you have not, and are using a television set, you could face up to a one-thousand-pound fine. If you're in there without one we'll know! Every time your doorknocker goes, you'll jump out of your skin, we know YOU'RE IN THERE!!!

From the electric to the gas, once they're in there they're gonna bust your ass and leave your house all cold and dark after they've cut you off for non-payment; you'll be better off living in the park, feeding on the ducks if you can catch one. But now if you can find one pound a week to spare, there might not be a need to tear out your hair because the national lottery is here to shower you with riches beyond compare, if only your six numbers can tear themselves away from the other forty three, and come out first; then the fates may do their worst. It's almost impossible to go broke when you're a multi millionaire unless your new and vast fortune is lodged in a bank where the speculators minds go blank when they're playing the numbers game, and they don't regain consciousness until, with a nasty shock, a line comes up on screen which says, "YOU MUSTN'T HAVE ANOTHER GO UNTIL YOU GET MORE DOUGH TO BACK YOU UP, GO BACK DOWN THE SNAKE TO WHERE IT SAYS START!" (And from there we strongly advise you to depart to a country that doesn't have an extradition treaty with your native land, and a cash flow problem too. And arrive with a few sets of hand luggage filled with loot, cocking a snoot from that safe haven at the suckers you've left behind you).

....
.....

QUIET WORLD.
94/95

There's no money to be made from reading, unless you're poised in front of a computer screen with your fingers ready to tap out decisions that can destroy people's lives, (people you've never seen and who have no substance for you), almost as fast as the facts and figures appear. You're a big wheel on the stock exchange this year, a roulette player by any other name, arrogance where there ought to be shame. And when you're forced to quit the ring, a burnt out but opulent thing, you might have a bad case of hyper-acusis to treat, and drag yourself off to a Buddhist seat of learning, where they'll draw out the poison with quiet soothing words. And slowly but surely, you'll learn to hear and love the songs of the birds as they greet the day in your cloistered grounds; there are few sounds that can work so sweetly on tortured nervous systems and send healing balms deep into the soul, and it's absolutely FREE!
Unless man destroys the global environment through his rampant GREED! And now perhaps that you've been flung off the whirling money-go-round, albeit with a tidy sum, you'll feel the need to buy a home in a silent dormitory village somewhere, and buy a computer so you can sit and stare at the insanity flashing across its screen at

the speed of light, and nod sagely and think, "They're all in for a terrible fright," but by then it will be far too late. And when you're in your bed at night the unbidden thought pops up,
"Fuck it, as long as I'm alright."

....

TERMINAL TEDIUM.
94/95

I wish I could feel the enthusiasm necessary to be a mountain molesting moron, or more relevantly, one of the stalwarts who have to go looking for them in hellish conditions. Or else, water skiing on an otherwise peaceful lake, disrupting life for everything left in my wake. Or maybe breaking the land speed record was meant for me, getting up to 700mph in as many seconds, and home in time for tea, passing myself on the way in to my hermetically sealed, solar-heated house, where thanks to triple glazing it's as quiet as a mouse recovering from a nervous breakdown after nearly being run over by a blue streak. "What a geekish thing to do" I sigh, as I yawn and blink my one good eye, and hope to die peacefully in my sleep. But why do I feel guilty when most 'manly pursuits' leave me cold? It's true I'm becoming

older with each passing year, and more arthritic too I fear. I'd like to be the world's best sexothonist, but my locking hips and lack of pulling power would let me down; still, I can indulge my mental whims from the comfort of my ancient armchair, eyeing up females on the TV who can't look back at me, only to give me the thumbs-down, as often happens when I solemnly perambulate around the town doing my shopping. I'd like to sleep the sleep of the 'too tired to be bothered', and on my headstone the epitaph: 'ON THE BRINK OF LIFE HE HOVERED'. Yeah, perhaps a spot of white water rafting would perk me up, 'it's less bovver wiv a hovver', you know, gliding over the rapids on a protective cushion of air, thinking vapidly, "I don't care if this goes on forever and I never get there."
("It's less bovver wiv a hover" as in hover craft or mower.)

……………………………………………..

DANGEROUS DETRITUS.
94/95

I'd like to be an eco warrior, but I've got too many disabilities to risk mixing it with thinly disguised psychotic security guards, hired by the combine. Most motorists are the Devil's disciples, evil predatory monsters who love belching out fumes of poisonous filth, this 'hot rails to hell' attitude accords with their idea of machismo. Many of them are frustrated 'RAMBO's or 'TERMINATOR's or EVEN WORSE!; when all they really are, are mental defectives racing and roaring round in murdering high-powered wheelchairs. Lobbing their effluent out the windows, gobbing on mere wimpish existence; too well hung to live peacefully, too crass to want to die in their beds at a decent old age.

The audacity of these metal wasps knows no limit, you can see one of them planted on the virgin turf of a huge rock pinnacle jutting out of the ocean, put there we're led to believe by the ad men, by divine right. I believe there's one even 'buried' on Ben Nevis, after it got stranded there. I wonder if its ghost terrorises climbers? Like some kind of abominable snowmobile, and that's why so many of them FALL OFF! And how canfilm director's salve their consciences after they've sent juggernauts hurtling down cliff faces, bursting into flames and leaving debris spread over a wide area? Or are those stunts done in miniature, and my fears unfounded? All I know is that this perverted lust for licence and liberty is stinking and sicking up the world; and yes, we are doomed unless.......

....

June, 95.

FROM FEAR TO ETERNITY.   1995.

There'll never be a convenient moment to die in; it's going to be a bit of a bore, running out of excuses to keep the grim reaper from my door. My chief reasons for wanting to put it off for as long as possible, is that I'm an atheist and don't believe in an after life; and love to go lusting after adorable women, with a view to turning at least one of them into a wife and mother to all my aches and pains, head cook and bottle-washer, and also prime keeper of her lord and master's drains.
Of course, I'm only joking; the last bastion of sanity left open to a totally 'new' man. I'd be so attentive to her every need, I'd even warm her feet with a warming pan after she came home from a hard day at the office, suffering from a bad case of cold and tired seat; whispering softly in her ear, 'What would you like to eat my dear, a soupcon of vegetarian stew, strained through a muslin sheet'?
Maybe I'll end up courting death? Trying to win it over with my most seductive smile, intoning huskily, 'If you'd care to wait I'll be with you in a little while, but if you've more urgent calls to make, you might be making a big mistake hanging around waiting to take me; I'm running a really tight schedule and you've dropped in completely

unannounced, with a look in your skeletal eyes that says you've already pounced on quite a few unsuspecting victims today. I really am rather busy you know, I wish you'd go away and take that grimacing leer off your skull while you're about it. It's no wonder you've got no friends; you look like my worst scenario for depression, a case that never ends. I see you when I wake up screaming, having escaped your scheming clutches by the skin of my teeth; and if I go for a swim in murky waters you're always lurking about, your eyeless bonehead hovering near, so that I come spluttering to the surface uttering a scream of primal fear.'

I suppose really I should go and see a shrink, who'll hypnotise me and put me at my ease, then when I'm at my lowest ebb of resistance you'll come crawling out of your spider's web hidden in the deepest recesses of my brain; growing ever bigger, fatter, hairier, hissing, 'Once more I've come for you again'. Reaching out with pincer-like tentacles to hold me in place so you can suck out my life's blood through my face! And as I watch myself writhing on the psychiatrist's couch, squirming and retching and gagging with pain, your greasy hiss snake's out to me, moaning 'There's no escape this time, it's a sealed room, you're securely locked in'. And as my body withers and shrivels to a mummy-like husk, you take on your final hideous shape. With a darting tongue to sense out where I am in the air, I see the gaping

black hole leading to your maw, knowing I'm destined to rot in there for evermore.
(PS. One of my unsuccessful entries to the 'Arvon' poetry competitions, there's one this year but I don't think I'll grace them with any of my superior efforts. 6/6/02)

....

G J W A. (GRAPE JUICE WITH ALCOHOL.) 24/12/90

If at first sleep doesn't succeed...then sleep some more...if you can get off again that is. Yet if sleep doesn't succeed at all, and you haven't got the courage to go OUT THERE!...Then I haven't really got any advice left to offer you; except perhaps to drink some more wine in the dead of night if your stomach can stand it. On certain nights where I live there's a breeze blowing or the wind is up, or it's raining, and when I go for a piss at 3am, I can tune into the sounds of the natural night. Nature is attempting to clean up after one more soulless, dirty human day, but the culprits will be up and about again long before Nature can hope to have any real effect; she's under contract to a multi national company called 'NEGLECT'; they're giving her more work to do for less pay,

they don't give a shit, they think she can be replaced.
Ah, but she makes the sweetest sounds at 3am, there's nothing to compare with them unless I hit upon a really good dream where disbelief is totally suspended, and participation is all that counts. Those few dreams are so precious and rarely remembered, or even glimpsed.
I could live permanently at 3am, there are seldom any people around then, and in summertime I could lie beneath the stars, and forget about this world of cars and the lunatics that guide them.

………………………………………………………..

CAR MANIA.
11/12/11/94

OK! Cars are convenient, cars are handy, they're even useful if you're feeling randy; (but they ain't got no culture, they even lack motivation if they run out of petrol, 5 miles from the nearest garage.) And you can manoeuvre the object of your desire onto the back seat and press home love's inclination between her parted feet, which are squashed up against the side windowpane; while her knees are digging into your waist and your balls are jammed up beneath her cunt and the windows become more misted up with every grunt.

Your straining cock pushes up inside her belly, the confined space becomes intimately smelly. You both want to fuck and fuck and have multiple orgasms and not die of exhaustion or ecstasy. Her love juice is streaming down over her arse and your taut scrotum, you want to get down and lick her off but that would disrupt this delicious motion; you've never known it to be this wild, the moon lights up your combined lust. Her vagina sucks on your cock with every thrust. Each kiss you plant on her mouth has a revitalising effect and nibbling on her nipples keeps them erect... Well, nothing can last forever; you're just on the 'vinegar strokes' and about to come together when there's a sharp tap on the side window and a too bright flashlight shines blindingly in. 'Excuse me sir, but you're holding up the traffic, we've had a complaint. I suggest that in future you exercise more restraint when waiting for a motorway breakdown van; I'm your friendly AA man and quite frankly I don't know where to put my face. The police have been videoing you for the last ten minutes, with a view to prosecution for your blatant display of selfish enjoyment. You could have caused a major accident as vehicles swerved around you. But they're saying it's the best blue movie there's ever been, and you both deserve a round of applause. So put your clothes back on right away and get moving without a pause, don't worry, your faces will be blotted out when this appears on the screen of every TV set of every police canteen... You should have seen the look on your face sir when I shone my torch right in, you looked like a man who's just been castrated, totally bereft of reason; your girlfriend looked pretty sick too. Go on, clear off the pair of you before I bill you for wasting my time'.

....
....

**WHY HAS THE BLUE FAIRY FORSAKEN ME? Or, MELODRAMA WILL NEVER BE DEAD AS LONG AS I'M ALIVE.
1/1/95.**

Plucked untimely from merciful sleep after less than seven hours of fitful slumber, I lie miserably awake, dreading whatever harassment the day may bring; most immediately in the guise of my 'neighbour's' kids, who might descend like the tribe of anthrax to play in their back garden soon, only a few feet away from my bedroom window. My spirits cower in mortal fear of any potential onslaught; if only my true love was lying beside me now instead of in the arms of another, I wouldn't need to take a possibly addictive tranquilliser to ease my pain and sense of foreboding of nervous disaster.

An event that would leave my brain in plaster, and my flimsy world in tattered shreds. All I want to do is escape into a haven of green warmth, a prenatal bower, but the slightest hollow thud, sounding like a ball being bounced, tips me brutally out of my dark retreat, feeling like a cornered animal. This morning they are all false alarms, which only make me feel worse, and want to escape even more...

00.05am, Jan 1st, 1995. One more new year welcomed in on my own, unless you count sharing it with a TV audience. There's fuck all to celebrate anyway, the grim life struggle continues unabated. It's disturbing that even though I'm 'free', I'm horribly trapped as well. Whenever I feel afraid I want to disappear deeper into nothingness, to have no contact from outside and ideally, only be comforted by someone who loved and understood me; and 'she' is always ministering to someone somewhere else, which only intensifies my isolation. Going for a piss at 00.40am, I hear a couple of giggly, pissed-up females pass noisily beneath my bathroom window; their voices are the siren's song, a clarion call to a pagan bacchanal, shagging lustily in the phosphorescent light of a full moon...but these images and urges fade with their voices. Experience has taught me that even if I'd chased out after them, one look at me and they'd have sobered up immediately, and gone on the defensive. Fucking lousy bitches! Or perhaps I'm wrong? Maybe if I'd caught up with them and wished them "Happy new year girls", they'd have

responded appreciatively to my slightly askew and aslant manly gaze, and beckoned me on to kiss them quick; shouting shortly afterwards at my retreating back, "Is that the best you can do, Reggie no dick?" And the moon would reflect off my glasses lenses, hiding the insane reaction inside my eyes. I flick the drops off the end of my penis, thinking disillusionedly, "Who needs 'New Year's' anyway?"
(PS 'Reggie no dick' was a reference to Reginald Christie, the mass murderer of 10 Rillington Place.)

....

I NEED AN EXPLANATION.
Winter 94/5

Her hair was the colour of autumn leaves, her temperament? Cold as the darkest winter's night, she was the last person to break my heart. Well, if life refuses to come to you, and your way to it is blocked by mindless adversity, what can you do? Find somewhere quiet to live, a seaside town like Whitby or St Ives, and bury yourself in an off-season let, for the 6 to 8-month winter duration.. Go down and listen to the eternal sound of the waves, suppress the most painful memories, locate

the cheapest places to frequent; dingy book shops, musty-smelling charity shops, cafes where they don't like too many customers, and dimly lit pubs where you can cry in your beer.
Where you choose to live has to be almost ghostly quiet, for those dark grey days when your bone-weary tiredness won't allow you to get up and go wandering around the town. On those days all you want to do is hide in sleep, or think about anything that might have a glimmer of warmth in it; were you born just to die alone? And on the days when you can go out and do your careful shopping, your sadness is intensified at the sight of all the healthy, good-looking people, who seem to have the life you crave so intensely. You feel like a reluctant outsider, and your self-pity turns to resentment and hostility.

....
......

LONELINESS.
20/21/6/94

I sit on the pavement beneath the all night, bright neon sign that advertises the closed laundrette; it's beautiful luminous colours attract me like a moth to a flame. I've been walking dimly lit streets for hours, looking for a tavern where I might hear the strains of 'THOSE WERE THE DAYS' by Mary Hopkins floating out the door. Instead, all I've sensed is an atmosphere of quiet unease; a combination of fear from urban terrorists, plague blight, and political correctness.

Soon, I'll lie on the pavement and hopefully sob myself to sleep; the cavalcade of insane motorists isn't due to start up for a couple of hours yet. Stretching out on the glowing sidewalk I imagine myself to be on a mortuary slab, the cold seeps into my head and body. A thought crosses my mind, or rather, a question, "Was I born just to die alone like this?" A couple of tears drip down my face, the relief of crying silently is almost comforting.

I can't look to my past for warmth or solace, most of my memories are painful and embarrassing; I have no future except to merely exist up to death sighs. I could hang on out of a sense of spite towards the State, which is my anonymous benefactor; if I die now I'll save its begrudging purse thousands. I want to fantasise about a green oasis in the midst of this emotional desolation, and populate it with women I've loved but have been rejected by; I've never known love. In the dream I have three lovers and they come to me as lovers, all pain and misunderstanding is erased. I fall asleep gratefully. I'm awakened by the traffic's roar, a WPC stands over me speaking into her 'walkie-talkie', I can't help noticing that she has nice legs.

....

PASSIVE 'SOAPS' STRESS OVERLOAD.
26/6/94

I can't comprehend how people can kill, rape, and pillage, yet I know how easy it is to hate. Fascists swear the 'holocaust' never happened; perhaps those starving African babies are nothing more than shrunken holy men fasting. "They've only got themselves to blame", my uncaring inner voice derides as I demolish my latest family-size pizza. "They make me sick, I wish they'd take their fucking problems elsewhere". It could never happen here; what's this headline in my local rag: 'GIRL KNOCKED OUT COLD IN COWARDLY ATTACK', and only last week some guy was jailed for rape, and this is only a 'sleepy backwater' village!
These late availability holidays seem really tempting; it's a pity I don't have anyone to go with. Women are all the same, only after one thing...your cash! Bleed you dry then cast you aside like a used condom. God! It's all so depressing, who needs it anyway? You only get one life, I'd like to spend mine feeling gay in the

old fashioned way; gosh, what an un-cool thing to say; you use public toilets at your peril these days, "A cottage made for two" is written on the wall of a stall in my blighted local 'john'. Going, going, gone is the peaceful life, when your neighbour can cut his privets with an electric carving knife that emits a jet engine's whining roar.

I need passive 'soaps' stress overload in my life because my own reality is so tame, "Gudday mate, no wurries cobber. Anyone want to buy a charnel house?" (It was originally proposed to sell Fred and Rose West's killing ground (their former home), until common decency prevailed and it was destroyed; now he's dead and she's caged for the rest of her natural.)   7/6/02

....

NONE TOO QUIET ON THE DOMESTIC FRONT.   17/1/95

I saw a dead pig hanging out of the open back door of a meat delivery van that I passed on a bus yesterday; I only had a moment to register this gruesome spectacle. Tonight I saw a man who weighs 712 lbs (that's over six hundredweight!) on a TV programme called: 'THE LAST AMERICAN FREAK SHOW'. The pig looked as though it was asleep, suspended by its back legs. I've no idea what sex it was, and that thought has never occurred to me before; whether female pig bacon tastes any different to male pig bacon? It's not stated on the packets, and anyway, I've virtually stopped eating meat; though if I wasn't ultra-cholesterol conscious, I'd be a bacon and sausage fanatic, they're so quick and easy to cook, and the aroma of sizzling, frying bacon for me, is quite addictive.

Overweight Americans don't seem to care, these guzzling lardos are always there, on the Oprah Winfrey show or the Rikki Laike talk fest, opinionated sad bastards with the saturated fat hanging off their chests; wondering why they've been dumped or cheated on, their massive heads resting on their rippling chins. A lot of them seem rather slow, except when it comes to food, which never says no to a bout of comfort eating; chocolate can become a permanent substitute for sex. I wonder if fat, huge, or obese people ever go broke in America, and have to slim out on the street? Living off, or rather on, their fat reserves; taking up jogging from handout to handout, devouring the occasional street urchin when they can't face 'cold turkey' from lack of food again.

....

MY TELEVISION SET NEVER SAYS NO.
25/1/95

Unless my worst fears are realised and it 'conks out' just before an episode of Coronation Street is about to start. If that were to happen it would mean instant grief, misery, desolation and despair, and an unplanned early night....on my own! It's difficult to describe how much television has meant to me during my lonely life, it has probably saved it on several occasions; for me the TV is truly a box of magic tricks. (It's still the case 11 years on. 27/6/06.)

....

UNIVERSITY OF LIFE CHALLENGE.
19/1/95

Hi, this is Phil Fletcher, reading an old 'SANDMAN' graphic novel and listening to, and taping, R&B off the radio; also suffering mild abdominal discomfort after my recent evening meal. Hi again, this is Phil Fletcher drinking good English bitter at less than 50p a pint and savouring a crumbly piece of Red Leicester cheese, all in the comfort of my living room, watching expendable crap on the TV; soon I'll smoke a slim panatela and go to bed, after I've sprayed the room with 'wild fresia' air freshener to deaden the ammonia-like after smell of the cigar smoke, it's either that or leave the small side window open all night.

"DIE, HUMANS DIE!" is my battle cry. I think the intelligentsia should rise up and wipe out the brute beast in our species, ONCE AND FOR ALL! A culling programme to ensure that quality, and not mere quantity prevails; when 'THE GUARDIAN' reader turns...that's when the final revolution will begin. You may not think it's possible to kill someone with a rolled up newspaper, even if it is one of the 'heavies', but if it's wrapped round a steel bar or a baseball bat, then you're in for a nasty surprise if it smashes down on to your skull; and on the psychic command from me, that is exactly what will happen. The worms will turn and attack all forms of anti social behaviourists. From the turds who smoke in 'NO SMOKING' zones right up to 'fornicating' royals. Did you know that 'royal' spelt backwards, spells 'layor', which, with a little stretch of the imagination, can be pronounced 'LAWYER!' (And we all know what a tribe of conniving, inbred, rip-off merchants they are, don't we?)

Maybe Armageddon will start on a Sunday, when in lovely suburbia, anyone not seen to be either mowing the lawn or cleaning the car will be bludgeoned to death with a copy of 'THE

SUNDAY TIMES', which is heavy enough to fell an ox with a single blow.

....
...

ZONDO SQUAD, AUCHWITZ. (Leave all hope you who in here enter.) 26/1/95

I want to throw myself into this monstrous vat of bubbling, boiling human flesh, but I'm too afraid that my death won't be instantaneous enough. I yearn to attack and overpower one of the guards and wrestle his machine gun from his grasp, and then turn it on him, his mates, and all of us involved in this diabolical operation of dragging corpses who've just been gassed, over to this stinking pit and rolling them in. I'm too weak, too numb; some heroes follow the dead into the earth cauldron, I envy them. I wish my heart, lungs and brain would recoil and burst from a sense of absolute horror; but a vestige of sanity tells me none of this is actually happening, that I'm having a Dante-esque nightmare, and the only way I'll survive it is to pretend it's not really happening and that I'll soon wake up. I'm ravenously hungry, and horrified to find myself salivating from the aroma arising from the charnel pit. Some Zondo workers are skimming off buckets of boiling fat,

God knows, the slop they feed us is watery enough. It would be a final sacrifice of the dead if some of that fat found its way into our soup. One of the guards barks at me, and I speed up my work in HELL!!!

COMANCHE.
15/1/95

Stabbing chips with a fork while listening to cool jazz in the Hebden Bridge Trades Club, on an otherwise shite and miserable January Sunday afternoon. I'm on my third 'Spritza', and the effect has gone to my head. For a short time I'm almost overcome by a spasm of emotional pain, brought on by lighting a slim cigar. I have to do a session of instant self analysis to bring me out of it in time to applaud the closing number of the excellent Mike Outram quartet set; and then no choice but to wend my litter-strewn way home alone, sorely in need of a piss.
What is it about me that decrees I should always be so lonely? I wipe the pots when I get in, and then give in to temptation and open a bottle of my dwindling wine stock; the call of 'DOCTOR WHO AND THE DALEKS' isn't strong enough for me to sit soberly, meekly awake in front of the TV set. I'm even prepared to sacrifice 'THE ANTIQUES ROAD SHOW' in favour of a couple more glasses of wine and a smoke; and then going for a lie down; falling asleep listening to RADIO 4. I wake up about 90 minutes later in the dark. Thank fuck

the radio's on, it brings me back to my senses quickly; I might as well switch to RADIO 1 to catch the last hysterical moments of this week's TOP40, 'REDNEX' is still the punters No. 1 choice, a completely mindless lyric; I have a blinding headache while I'm penning this empiric.

....

SNIPPETS OF FRAGMENTS.
20/9/94

Charlie likes the dawn best of all, he lives far enough from civilisation not to have the misfortune to hear any of its mechanical sounds, or inflame his lungs with its chemical odours. He loves to hear the cry of the Curlew across the open moor as he takes in lungfuls of dew soaked air; wishing that summer lasted much longer. In his early morning compulsion he often walks his horse into the village; it's iron shod hooves make a tremendous clatter along the cobbled main street, there have been angry mutterings to have him banned before 8am. He can't forgive fate for allowing him to be born nearly four centuries too late. He detests this modern era as much as Roundheads hated Cavaliers. Anathema wasn't enough to sum up the contempt he felt for this soulless and lazy age of tarmac and tourists.

"People have lost the ability to exist alone" he thought. Today there's this great surging need to be together, the weekend hordes of motorised lemmings following each other on the road to 'THE DEVIL'S KITCHEN'. Well they do do a nice homemade scone and a pot of Earl Grey there at a very reasonable price, if you've the patience to wait up to half an hour to get served".

21/9/94. They say there's someone for everybody, he'd turned down the one who was on offer for him a good few years ago. She'd been too seriously facially challenged for him to get used to, and the idea of living with a woman who weighed more than he did turned him off altogether; after all, she might have continued to expand whilst basking in the glow of his largesse...what a hideous prospect! He likened himself to Vincent van Gogh and Heathcliff, having the tortured desire of the first for a blissful physical union, and the smouldering resentful brooding of the second for being denied his 'Cathy'. He didn't like to be crossed either in love or anything else, he had stylishly renamed himself 'Vincent Heathcliff', and circumstances were forcing him to live up to his new name; he strongly suspected that Heathcliff died from nervous exhaustion, a fate he expected to share.

(From around the same period). " Dear God, why don't you exist? If you existed, would you have allowed me to drop my typewriter last Thursday afternoon, only a couple of hours after I'd had a new ribbon put in, leaving it with a broken arm? I really liked that machine as well; it was so compact and suited my needs admirably. I could have gone anywhere in the world with it and set up shop. Portable typewriters are becoming one more endangered species; I'll miss the cut and thrust of hammering out the grapes of wrath on its trusty keys. Knock three times on the ceiling if you do exist, not too loudly though, I've only just had it retiled with polystyrene squares".

....

MOMENTS OF CLARITY. (For Vincent van Gogh, and me.)   12/5/94

The death of hope, and the birth of a dull acceptance that I can't find love; or worse, that I'm to be denied it. Better to be born any other creature than human rather than endure this fate; to be here once in all eternity and experience every emotion other than the deepest one there is...? Better to be a creature purely in tune with the elements, and whose main concern is to procreate before dying, than to suffer the pangs of unfathomably cruel and continuous rejections. I'd rather be a lone male tiger with merciless teeth and claws, a beautifully developed mixture of appetite and indolence. To eat for as long as I'm able to hunt, and to drink, only water and blood. As for loving, that would be controlled by a hierarchical status during a fixed mating seaso; or whether I could nip in quick and take advantage of some randy female while the local stud was otherwise engaged. I wouldn't be aware that the planet's in danger of frying, or that my species is being wiped out to feed Ignorance and Superstition. I'd just prowl about beneath a forest moon and swipe at glinting stars in forest pools.

···

GREYING WITH RAGE.
16/11/94

Oh, why can't I feel forgiving when it comes to forgiving you? My mind feels as black and menacing as a huge anaconda snake towards you. We should be enjoying our love but you've withdrawn my visiting privileges; you've become coy and aloof, the colour of dust. When I first met you, you had radiantly coloured hair, like a blending of amber and musk oil catching the sunlight; then inexplicably you hacked off those wonderful lustrous locks, leaving your hair a cropped mess, a spiky frizzed orange. Probably I should have become wary of you then, but I was terribly alone and at least you would talk to me, and listen and remember. You wanted me to fall in love with you so you could use it against me, so I'd end up standing out in the night trying to fathom out what could be going on behind your tightly drawn curtains, a hunter's moon picking me out among the shadows.

I'd hang around till your lights were extinguished, then let the street lamps guide me home. I love the luminous glow they lend to pavements and walls; this time last year you and I were on holiday in Cornwall, we were amazed at how green and alive and clean the foliage looked in winter, and the sea, sand and sky were in close harmony, all freshly laundered. On our first night there we walked down to the beach, you played your guitar to a song you'd written about yearning for passion and hunger; the breakers came gliding in quite gently. I said, "Listening to the waves breaking is like listening to eternity, this sound will go on forever", not realising that I'd be so temporary in your scheme of things. The sting in your ostracism of me is as poisonous as deadly nightshade, my cruel Belladonna.

....

A HEROIC SACRIFICE OF BRAIN CELLS.
26/11/94

Farewell to mere mortality, I've shrugged it off at last, and risen above political correctness to become a lambasting iconoclast. Goodbye to poetry 'comping', may their organisers rot in hell, and their judges deliberate eternally on the most putrefying sulphurous smell.

....
....

UNREST IN PIECES. Unrest in pieces William Shakespeare, I hope you've spun yourself to shattered fragments in your grave at the abysmally poor performance that good Sir Luvvy gave in 'AS YOU LIKE IT/MEASURE FOR MEASURE'. It caused 'THE GUARDIAN' critic much too much displeasure, he said, "Never before has the bard been brought into such disrepute, unless you count the time when his 'RICHARD 111' was played by a vertically challenged dromedary in a suit". Alas good Sir Luvvy is 'Learing' all the way to the bank.

A FAREWELL TO ARTHRITIS-FREE ARMS. Gone for good is my no cost health care, it's gone forever along with the natural dyes in my hair. Now, I'm reminded with every step I take, that my hips and knees have lost their pep; and my lungs heave and strain every time I struggle uphill in the rain. No luxury of car driving for me, my eyes are too weak to see, and my mind too infirm to grasp the complexities required for this high-risk task. It takes me all my time to stop my gob opening and closing like that of a landed fish, while I'm waiting for a bus; and to exercise my brain takes a lot of aches and pain.

Still, galloping middle age has its compensations, no more of those squirmingly embarrassing conversations necessary to chatting young women up, now it's strictly 'grab a granny' night for me; or watching 'Corrie' on TV. I'd start writing my memoirs, except it's far too late, nothing ever happened in my life that I want to relate, this piece says it all.

(I know we all like to revel at other's misfortunes, especially me; luckily I've managed to pull myself back from the steep precipice of despair that I was destined to jump off, here in the UK, and give myself a new stab at life, although a perverse fate still stalks me wherever I go. But I don't intend to die here, cold and alone. 27/6/06.)

VIRTUAL REALITY, IT'S ALMOST EVERYWHERE.   14/5/93.

Masturbation is all that there is for me, but when I think of you it's virtual reality. And as I sit here, home alone in my rocking chair, it gives me a bit of a scare the way my favourite TV programmes come round so quickly, the seven-day cycle in only 7 minutes. Poetry's fucked as far as I can see, nothing new to say, with a thousand different ways of saying it; literary snobs dominating the 'Lit Supp's. Sylvia Plath was the last real poetess, and she's been dead since 1963; but then of course there's always me.

I long to be esoteric but it's not to be; I'm not well versed enough in obscurity. And yet the need to create is never ending, a compelling force from within; the urge to go on and on in an untried and undisciplined manner, an overwhelming desire to 'come of age';

to combat the futility of my existence by using the written page. Believe me, it is futile, apart from hope; I'm the original dope on a rope, a person with disabilities and hang-ups to match, a rejected candidate for the booby hatch. Is it politically incorrect to use such a term? I hope so, I'd rather be anything than a non-judgemental worm; oh blandness forgive me.

I could bang on about the state of the planet, but I'm not starving to death right now, Goddamn it! And I've got enough OXFAM jumpers for each day of the year; Tigers are down to their last 5 thousand in the wild I hear? (I wonder who counted them?) And walking for the whales along the Rochdale canal seems tame somehow, compared to what 'THE SEA SHEPHERD's prepared to do, (although I've never actually heard of anything that this fabled eco warrior ship has actually done.) I wonder if it could support a few dolphins instead of lonely swans? (The Rochdale Canal that is.)

Maybe they could be trained to tow the water bus, that would save cyclists without permits, the irksome bother of having to make detours round the piles of horse flop, and narrowly miss tipping harassed walkers like me into the cut: (the water bus has long since gone.)
Yes, Sylvia Plath has said it all, she's left me feeling intellectually small; it's a pity she didn't stick around long enough to get cured of her depression; I wouldn't have minded sitting at her feet at Lumb Bank, or Totliegh Barton. I also wish I was a wood carver and not a writer, I could then be thinking in eons when it comes to leaving something worthwhile behind me. Images of late twentieth century decadence, (always other people's never my own, I am without, [I cannot be serious surely? 'I am without', what the fuck's that all about?]) captured in oak; recycling church pews yanked out of mouldering churches. My chisel's moulding the curves of licentious bodies in lewd and lascivious acts; the sort of artwork I look for in graphic novels amongst the blood and guts, and morbid prose. Speaking of which, I've failed to find one, a 'pro' that is, with whom I could get it on when the mood and the 'in funds situ' took me. 'JUST FOR MEN', is the hair colour restorer that I use, it makes me feel rejuvenated every six weeks or so; though it stinks a bit the first couple of times you wash your hair and blow dry it afterwards. But if I had to choose between a bit of a pong and a 'salt and pepper' thatch, I'd catch my breath

dramatically and rush towards the nearest mews, and piss up against its well appointed wall.
(If my memory serves me well, the above was my '93 entry for the Arvon Poetry Comp'; with hindsight I can see that it might have trod on a few corns. But hey! what the fuck! I don't give a damn. Serves them right for taking an entrance fee off a poor disabled writer; I also reckon that Ted Hughes matched Sylvia Plath's cosmic bleakness in 'BIRTHDAY LETTERS'. I've never really understood why 'normal' people can be depressed, most of mine has sprung from my physical plight, life should be for living and loving, not being gratuitously miserable.)   8/6/02

....

WINDOW SHOPPING
23/1/93

A projected view from my imaginary French windows would be, in the immediate foreground, a well tended lawn bordered by flower beds, shrubs and trees; following on from these would be open, rolling fields, with woodland copses interspersed, and on the horizon, the sea. On summer nights I'd be able to sit out on my lawn and contemplate the mysteries of the heavens, and trace the course of

the moon as it traversed the night sky; illuminating the ground and the ocean. I'd be able to sit out for as long as I liked, something I can't do where I live now, as there are too many people and dogs in the neighbourhood, to send my paranoia and resentment levels soaring.
Whenever I see the full moon outside my window, I always feel like drinking wine; there should be a special sensation about moonlit nights; I feel I should be out walking, preferably a bit stoned and sizzled. But unless I have the privacy that I long for, a deep desire to be away from prying eyes and minds, I will sullenly sit inside my prison-like home that this noisy, over active world has made for me, and mourn over the death of mysticism. By 'mysticism' I don't mean witchcraft, it has more to do with a harmony with Nature; even the night has deep colours when the moon is up. Something I miss in my present situation is being able to see the stars, once again, if I stand out in my front or back garden for too long, I feel I'm under surveillance and my motives misunderstood. Also the stars aren't too easy for me to pick out, as I'm visually handicapped. The last time I saw a night time sky filled with stars was fifteen years ago, when I was travelling through Greece; a small group of us was hitching across country and we were forced literally to bed down by the side of the road one night. I woke up before dawn and watched this age-old spectacle at my leisure, I remember watching the night recede until the bright glow

from the planet Venus was diminished by the encroaching daylight. We were making for Sparta.

....

PSYCHEDELIA.
20/1/93

Audio bass caressing distressed emotions, Fender guitars heavenly instrumental journeys, Karmically liberating musical notes, opiates. Paradisical quest, reviving, serene, tender, Unwanted vexations, waning Xoanon yearning zenith.

....

CAVE MOUTH.
Early '90s

It isn't death that I long for, only black ease; like the night, the starry night. The night and the deep orange glow of street lamps, and elemental Nature in all her moods. I'm not afraid of the night, only people; the night would never hurt me, it doesn't even notice me. Even in her wildest frenzies,

Nature isn't directing her wrath at me, I'm as relevant to her as a single drop of rain, or a leaf torn from a tree. The night doesn't mind my loneliness, won't shun or despise me because of it; it will not deny me access, it will even encourage me to go walking beneath her moonlit canopy. And if, at anytime I managed to walk beyond mere mortality, past the range of orange street lights to where the moonlight was as bright as day, and I found a cave mouth up in some sandy foothills, I'm certain that Nature, the mother of night, wouldn't mind me taking up residence just inside the entrance. She might even send night breezes to soothe my pain away, caresses freely given. There are few things that compare with the smell and touch of pure air brushing your cheek late at night, with the sound of rippling water running from a stream nearby, and the breeze gently brushing the leaves on the trees. If I ever found myself in such a place, I would want to start to forget the bitterness, the hatred, and the horror of a disappointing life. I would sit or lie, just inside the cave, not caring about sustenance, except for water. And even if it took forty days and forty nights, I would achieve my goal to find complete forgetfulness.

To be left alone, no more intrusive than murmuring laughter, or like water in a stream, or as inconspicuous as a grain of sand; as harmless as a sunbeam reflected in that stream...And if, in a few thousand years time, my skeleton was unearthed from its winding sheet of sand, and a new human picked up my skull in his or her warm, intelligent hands, she or he might well say, "This man died laughing".

....

I'M FIFTY, GOING ON THIRTY-FIVE.
(There's a bit of a violent mood swing here.)
22/2/97

Hey, I feel dead fit me, like a dog with two dicks. I'm always on the sniff, I could go through a large section of the female population, say 16 to 55 (only the fit ones at the latter end), at a rate of knots; I'm a knickers-sniffing kind of man that's what I am. Some people say I look like 'DESPERATE DAN' because of my boring granite jaw, well I can assure you it's not 'cow pie' that turns me on, 'finger pie' would be nearer the mark. On the remote chance that I might have some girl lying stark naked in the dark in bed next to me, then all I'll want to do is stick my fingers up her flue just for piss-flap openers, PPPPHHHHWWWWOOOO-AAAARRRR!!!! When it comes to a quick fifty off the wrist, I'm a consummate artist, the secret is to make the foreplay last as long as possible by fantasising about some wench who won't come across with the

goods; this can make you come with loads of spunk if you're not 'bashing the bishop' every night; the higher it spurts the greater your delight. "Not bad for an old git", you end up saying, while laying your hand on something to wipe it off, a dead baby's removal cloth. Yeah, I still feel dead fit for fifty me, thank fuck I've still got my own hair, even though it looks like a 'syrup of figs' ('wig' for anyone who's never been exposed to cockney rhyming slang), I wish I was a gynaecologist able to examine vaginas in the stirrups..."
(From the somewhat egotistically enlarged author of : CAVE MOUTH.?)

....

THE LUCK OF GOOD LOOKS.
30/6/97

When you're young and good-looking, you can be anonymous in a nice sort of way, approving glances and comments can make your day; men want to adore and open doors for you, your looks can be worth their weight in gold. But today's modern girl is rewriting the code, confusing the male instinct to love, own and possess, body and soul; till on the whole neither side knows where they stand. Physical attraction is an addiction for me, even though good looks can be a total mirage and ultimately work against their owners.

I believe there's definitely something suspect about the identity of the Mona Lisa, that 'she' could be a transvestite in disguise, and that's what that famous smirk is all about. (Some informed people reckon it's a self-portrait of the artist, in drag.) You can get a nasty surprise if you take one of those home after a few drinks, assuming that 'her' smiles and winks are the prelude to a night of bliss, and 'she 'ends up saying, "Come on big boy suck on this!" (Well, if no-one's going to find out...) Of course there are evil monsters out there who think they must have a pretty girl at any cost, the name of Ted Bundy springs to mind, his method of seduction was invariably the lethal kind. Beauty is indeed only skin deep, and I have often cried myself to sleep for the lack of it; many of those that have it think it's theirs by right, and not just a fortunate accident of birth; I've been the butt of mirth and derision for setting my sights too high, ogling beautiful women through my one good eye.

....

IN THE ABSENCE OF SEX
28/6/97

In the absence of good old-fashioned cathartic sex, I tend to eat to exsex, oops!, sorry, I mean excess; I've got sex on the brain. But I don't want to get spotty or fat, so I don't pig out on chocolate, I make sure of that. It's true that eating sweet things can soothe your fevered brow; biting into a succulent peach or apple can afford the same short term pleasure as a masturbatory climax, short and sharp; though I must admit I've never heard the playing of a harp while the juice is running down my chin. Laughter too is another safety valve, your tortured nerve endings it can salve, unless you've gone so long without sex you've become as shrivelled up and dry as a wrinkled old prune. And there's nothing more infuriating when you know perfectly well how to do it, to be subjected to the rigours of those who don't, or can't be bothered, even when their partner is swinging provocatively from the chandelier! No more day time TV phone ins for me, or I fear I might kick the screen in on my new 21-inch set, and I haven't even paid for it yet. Having sex on the brain can be painful too, walking round with a seven- inch erection poking through your skull could lead to the social ostracism of you in this sexually sensitive age; when overt male sexuality can lead to direct female outrage. 'PRIDE AND PREJUDICE' has got a lot to answer for when it comes to the false morality of sexual repression; I was once told when I was young, and gasping for it, to go and buy a pound of liver and stick my knob in that, it resembles an unwelcoming twat; and I could fry it up for my tea afterwards with a bit more protein in it than it previously had.

....
...

FIVE MILES DOWN. By the 'matt black' Phil Fletcher.   **26/8/96**

The root of my soul lies five miles down, life goes on there but not as you could begin to understand it. It's a world of absolute blackness and silence, the pressure is so intense it would squash lesser mortals like slugs; you can only hope to survive it if you know how to protect yourself. Monsters abound in that black ink, so primitive they haven't learnt to think, just gaping black holes in an even denser one, where creatures are sucked in with no hope of ever getting out. Black death sludge bubbling at the base of the world

....

OTHER PEOPLE ARE MY HANDICAP.
22/4/97

I feel pressure on me to go insane because of the inane response I get to the root of all my pain, namely, weak pig-like eyes hiding behind strong-lensed glasses... 'Ooh!' What a turn off apparently. And of course, it's all my own fault; I chose to look this way? When in fact I'd rather fade away because of the strain of this disability. As I get older the problem seems to be getting worse, I'm living in a schizoid state of unease, like a kicked dog cowering against another attack from someone's malicious mouth. How savagely ironic that I, a sycophantic worshipper of female, and sometimes, disquietingly, male physical beauty, should be cast down so low by my lack of it. Fifty years of life and I've never had a 'wife', realistically there's nowhere left for me to go, except where I might find a glow, or even a glimmer, of human sympathy.

....

FIRST VERSE LAST. (The last few lines were created 25 years ago ["Now perhaps..."] when I was coming down off an LSD trip.)
20/4/97.

Moving with rhythmic mystic motions out along the hidden shore, imbibing ancient magic potions so I can breathe way down on the ocean floor. Extreme water pressure has reduced my stature to a minute size, riding on a sea horse's back I'm able to see clearly into those black depths; this underwater night holds no fears for me, when it gets too bright we'll dive down into a deeper sea called eternity. Now perhaps that time has ended and my wounded soul ceases to dry out from pain, all the colours of life have blended to help me live in peace again.

....

A RAINY NIGHT IN THURSO.
22/4/97

A rainy night in Thurso, sitting in my hotel room, farting, wrinkling my nose up at the smell; thank fuck I brought a can of air freshener with me. I'm not feeling very well; on the horns of a dilemma, wondering what on earth to do, sit on my own in the resident's lounge, or watch snooker on BBC 2? Or even 'DR. DEATH', the euthanasia man, he's on the TV too. I think I'll drink the miniature bottle of whisky I bought in John o' Groats today; 5cls of 40% alcohol should chase my indecisiveness away.
I've decided on 'DOCTOR DEATH', I might learn something useful for a rainy day in Todmorden, a graveyard for lonely men like me.
(I actually knocked the 8-year old glass of malt whisky out of my hand, or rather, it felt as if my

hand was jerked upwards and it flew over my arm virtually untouched. I spent the next 10 minutes rubbing the dregs out of the carpet...)

....

I LEFT A MESSAGE ON YOUR ANSAFONE. 20/8/97

Looking through myself to the night beyond, I wish some thing could wave a magic wand and give my life back to me. There's nothing left but the will to live, and that's no excuse to stay alive; it's like existing in hell, with all that involves; no air to breathe, and only sulphur and hate to smell, and fear and horror to taste. How can such a pointless waste of a life be justified?
I'd rather be sitting on a desert rock with Don Van Vliet, founder of 'CAPTAIN BEEFHEART AND HIS MAGIC BAND', studying grey and white patterns beneath a full desert moon, and getting so stoned on the night breeze there'd be no coming back to my world of grey and black; and no death beyond. Maybe an aspect of Venus would materialise out of iridescent skies, and enfold me in her loving arms and never let me go out of her sight, and nurture me back to some kind of caring state through singing the song of the siren into my

tortured head. We could sleep in our bed of love till I, at least, was safely dead.

....

NICE-LOOKING PEOPLE.
27/8/97

I try not to offend the gaze of nice-looking people; I'm terrified of their disapproval. I squint longingly at the female ones through slits covered by disfiguring, bulbous-lenses specs; and one eye's bigger than the other and has a fixed stare, except when it's glaring out of the corner. But I do get sick of them making me feel nervous and insecure; I don't really want to be bothered with them anymore. After all, for a lot of them, their only claim to look down judgementally on me is that they're nice-looking and I'm not.
My face wrongly reminds them that there's another world out there, where nice-looking people don't voluntarily go; not if they want to come back alive that is. The blood red world of predator and prey. If only I had a nice-looking female as an ally to take the heat off me; while they're admiring her they're not focusing on me, except to wonder how I could have pulled such a

nice-looking plum. Well, I might be ugly, but I'm ALIVE!

I see nice-looking couples who have no energy or lustre, and no real notion of the depths of passion that nice looks or beauty can engender. There's slender little hope that I'll taste those fruits again in this image-conscious age; and being nice-looking is an automatic passport to the good life if you know how to use it. Existence should have a deeper meaning than this, but being nice-looking should lead to being in a state of bliss.

....

A FANTASTIC PHALLUS FOR FUCK-ALL. (It's alright ma, it's only words that I'm weaving.)

(I'm surprised I haven't dated this, but I'm fairly certain it's from around the same time as the above, I know I sent it out to some poetry mag' and they wrote back saying they couldn't publish it.)

Here-to-fore and therein after, let there be an end to laughter until I've won a BAFTA for my life story. It's a terrible thing to discover that you exist only inside a vacuum, a complete outsider except in the warmth and comfort of your living room.

Still, what the fuck, nothing says you'll be guaranteed good luck when you're born into this life. "This is your 'living hell' incarnation", I hear a voice inside me say. I mentally reply, "It could be made more bearable if you and your unholy host of cohorts would ride away into that black sunset that is your home, and leave me alone to roam the TV world that I love.

I wish I could live more like the other animals, living only to eat and shag, and being allowed to mate with your jaws still covered in blood and still-living tissue stuck to your teeth. (I'm sure I don't really, can you imagine the type of weirdo's these sentiments could attract? It doesn't bear thinking about. 29/6/06.)

Anarchy in the new way, the only allegiance you owe is to yourself; you want humanity to cop it really bad; when 200 Taiwanese fry-die in a distant land, whose ethics towards noble creatures you cannot stand, your only response is, 'Well, that's 200 less monsters to clamour for tiger-penis soup; they'll be able to loop-the-loop of insanity by instead savouring the flavour of crisply fried Taiwanese noodles'. (There was a plane crash there this week, killing all 200 on board.)

There's a road passes by my window and it's filled with growling, snarling, discontented cripples in their high-powered wheelchairs. I can feel their greedy need for a magic cure tear into my nerve endings as they drive uncaringly by. I wish they'd all die from inhaling the polluted air they suck in from each other's exhausts; automobiles are the most consistent killing machines of the twentieth century holocaust. I sincerely hope one of them doesn't catch me in its headlights one night, and snuffs me out before I have time to shout, "You mindless moronic bastard! I deserve much better than to be killed by you".

The savage 'old order' of the 'dream time' of Australia and the American west was the best'; those ancient people knew how to live in harmony with the planet; 'Civilisation'?, they began it. They didn't allow their inquisitiveness to run amok, they were too busy worshipping the Great God Cock and its equally fascinating counterpart Cunt; and venerating animals in the hunt, not just viewing them as commodities to be exploited to extinction. Of course, I don't mean any of this, this is merely a disenchanted diatribe, those ancient people's were always hounding each other to death, and you couldn't take a breath without having to thank some imp or demon for it; life's a pile of shite and then you die a harsh and lonely death; I should know, it's happened to me often enough.

....
....

HAPPY BEING MISERABLE.
16/12/97

It's a pity being miserable is considered to be such a social crime, because if it was otherwise, I could be happy being miserable most of the time. Cold sores can be a source of misery, especially when you have to appear in public for your tea, like me, right now on my 5-day, pre Christmas spree holiday, here in Exmouth. "Unclean, unclean! Ooh, where's your mouth been"? I can hear people scream at me, in a bad dream of unspoken accusations. The less that's actually said about this crusty excrescence, the more its presence is felt by me; it begins to throb and glower, dominating every waking hour, oh for the power of lip salve to remove it. But it's cold and wet outside, and the shops are three quarters of a mile away, and I don't know where the nearest Chemist's is, and it's already dark; I'll probably bump into lots of things along the way and when I finally get inside the shop my glasses will be all steamed up, and I'll have to take them off so that the young and lovely assistant (assumed) will see how ugly I really am. She'll hone straight in on the strawberry jam stain on my upper lip and pass me a tube of zit cream using the tips of her fingers with sterile plastic gloves on.

My anxiety and insecurity levels spin more and more out of control, on the whole this hasn't been one of my most enjoyable 'TINSEL AND TURKEY' do's, I even forgot my flask of 5-star French booze (brandy), so now I'm reduced to paying hotel prices for my cockle-warming tipple. I wonder why I get these mad impulses to socialise; when at heart I'm a social and emotional cripple? I'd be better off staying at home on my own where it doesn't matter if I've got a cold sore oozing yellow matter over the rim of my cup, and wincing each time the edge of a spoon catches this suppurating split in my lip as I'm spooning 'live' yoghurt into my mouth. Why 'live' yoghurt you may well ask? Well, the telling of the tale "Why"? is a task that I'm not up to performing; at least not in this abnormal genre. Er, sorry, I mean method of communication.

....

THE 8 MILLION POUNDS WANTED POEM.
15/12/97

Before you know it, two thirds of your life expectancy has gone; next year I'll be fifty-one; I'm only hanging on in the hope of some kind of miracle happening. I'm still searching for success to free me from the unwholesome mess that my life's in. Maybe I should place a begging ad in 'PRIVATE EYE', though I can't imagine anyone, short of being stark staring mad, bothering to reply. ('Help me to help myself to your cash…') I know I wouldn't. The cheeky fuckers! 'Sort code 36-24-36, account no: 3516243947', no gift too small.

Now, there's the ongoing phenomena of lottery millionaires, no more worries, no more cares, a whole new strata of anonymous rich bastards to envy and dote on; I think I'll put my coat on and go out and buy a ticket, after all, 'you've got to be in it to win it'. One 'lucky dip' and a merry quip to the wizard machine operator such as, 'I don't get out of bed for less than fourteen million, me'. I laugh about this smart remark all the way back to my squat in the now defunct 'parkie's' hut, in the run down park, after dark; hoping that the all night mobile security patrol won't spot me. Oh no, they've got me bang to rights, they're flashing blinding lights in my eyes and cursing, and dispersing my belongings amongst the ducks out on the half frozen lake. 'For pity's sake', I woefully cry. 'Without my sleeping bag I'll surely die of cold'. 'Tough shit', says the burly one with the gold ear-ring and the 'cut here' tattoo marked round his throat. 'I've a good mind to throw you in after it, you steaming pile of shite; an' I will an' all if we catch you here on any other night. You sad bastard 'paraffin lamps' are all the same, it's a shame we don't do what the Nazis did during the last war. Ethnic cleansing? I'd hold open the gas chamber doors and boot you in; I've a good mind to put one on your chin, I blame the government for the state this country's in'.

....
......

BLUES FOR THE MILLENNIUM
31/1/98

The great anti climactic countdown is already on, is it 2000 or 2001 when we're all supposed to go gaga and bow down to the new millennium dome? I'll be genuflecting from home, alone, in front of my TV, watching this massive excuse for a grope and a snog in Trafalgar and Times Square; pulling my party popper in my old rocking chair. And what will this brave new era hold for non-contributing specimens like me, who aren't able bodied enough to get on their bikes and go whizzing round looking for work? The global economy's already turning pear-shaped.
I'm too busy raging against my hair turning white, and determined not to go too gentle into that grey twilight of middle age dread, to overburden my head with these imponderables; no doubt the same 25% of humanity will have all the ' squanderables', while the rest of us are privileged to look on in envy. Perhaps we'll all be granted a new millennium medal and mug, with Tony and Cherie's faces smiling benevolently out at us through glaze and chrome, and the slogan, 'FORWARD FOREVER WITH NEW LABOUR' emblazoned on the people's glittering throne-dome; where the same over indulged few will be

invited to a slap-up do at single mother's welfare expense, or else ten pence on the council tax. If I could afford a fax machine, I'd send a real grumbler off to the queen along the lines of, "Dear your Maj', if the NHS is allowed to deteriorate any more, I doubt if I'll survive to reach three score years and ten, let alone my century in 2047, by which time you'll rightly be reigning in heaven; so who am I going to get my telegram from, Prince Charles's son? Or will you have been abolished by then and we all pay homage to number 10? I sincerely hope so. Yours, a disgruntled old armchair campaigner for disabled people's rights. If all your wealth and the cost of the dome were put together, then me and the other 6.5 million disabled burdens, could live forever on not-so-humble pie in the sky; which I'd like to see you try living on.
Yours, an anonymous benefits 'scrounger'.

....

(PS. Quite a lot of my predictions came true, I was on my own on the eve of the great non-event, and I'm still a burden on the state. PM Blair has very recently said he wants to see more and more of us in work, but what could I be eligible for? 55, severely visually handicapped, and at times severely emotionally handicapped as well, to the extent that I can hardly drag my carcass out of bed, and death seems like a soft option? Maybe I'll send him a copy of this completed book.) (29/6/06.

Tony's on the political ropes now, he's not even due to see out his 3rd term in office, and he's lost all credibility with me, his one-time biggest grassroots fan; and frankly my queer dear, I don't give a damn about the UK anymore, it's a burden and a chore being stuck here. Vincent Heathcliff.)

....

TURNING THE OTHER CHEEK
4/11/97

I need lots of sleep in the mornings, thank Christ I don't have a job to go to requiring me to get up. It's a terrible pity I don't have someone who adores me, to bring me tea in a loving cup about 10am, and gently remind me that if I'm not up and about in the next half hour, I'll miss Richard and Judy again. I usually turn over and bask in the golden warmth built up inside my bed, and push away from me the horrors of my life; and listen to 'WOMAN'S HOUR' instead.
We're taught from an early age that it's a sin to lie in bed, I only regard it as a sin against myself if I'm lying there too depressed to move, with never a soul coming near; but as an act of unashamed luxury it can only be surpassed by an unhealthy intake of tobacco, wine and beer; after which I

usually end up in bed again in a spaced-out state, till heavy slumber takes over and releases me for what feels like eight hours of a prelude to death; it's very rare that I dream during a drunken stupor. And in the dead silence of a Sunday morning, the full horror of my recent debauch is brought home to me by a host of imps and demons cavorting inside my head, each one representing an aspect of my personal failings. So, on this bed of nails I writhe, till I can stagger up and take five valerian capsules to ease my pain, swallowed down with the immortal words, "Never again, Oh God, never again".

(PPS. Only joking Mr Blair; you know I'd be out there busting my balls if I could, I mean, we can't all be lawyers can we? Making it up as we go along; the law is a law unto itself and a damned expensive one at that; the Masonic lodge of the legal profession? A bunch of twats and bastards if you ask me. Of course, I could be sued for slander and libel for these remarks, and they probably will if they ever see my work making any money; I'll probably lose my copyright to pay them off...WANKERS!!!!)

....

GHASTLY, VILE AND OBNOXIOUS ODOURS
11/1/98
('God's ultimate joke against man isn't sex, it's bad guts and sweaty feet.)

Why do our nostrils react so violently to the smell of sulphur and decay? We instantly waft them away with our faces all wrinkled up in agony. "It's not me", we all vehemently cry if the stench happens to be hovering nearby to where we're guiltily stood. Some misguided souls think that the sex act is their 'god's' ultimate joke against mankind, they couldn't be more wrong; you don't find many people laughing when the gassy aroma of your farts is too strong for them to breathe the same air as you. At least that smell will blow away if there's enough of an air current to shift it, but the odour of cheesy feet can't be beat for clinging power in a confined space, you can't get rid of it. And as for the odious fumes of bad breath! It's like having the cloying stench of death breathed into your face by, quite often, an unwitting purveyor; a slayer of elephants at fifty paces. What store can be put on social graces if your ancient hostess creaks with the reek of camphorated mothballs emanating from the long dead fox fur around her corded neck? The inflammable fragrance of firelighters is much more preferable, (not many people under thirty will have smelt either.) And the appalling odour of rotting fish leaves a lot to be desired; I don't think it's inspired many poets to flights of fancy, unless I think of Nancy the street girl, the gusset of whose tights had a lot in common with that once smelt, never forgotten pong. She'd have her head buried in her chest, sniffing patchouli oil on her vest, oblivious to requests of, "Close your legs Nance, your breath smells". Guaranteed to repel all boarders except the most sex-starved of tomcats, the fishy mating call of over-active female twats is one that gives me shagger's droop. I only ever smelt it once, as I held my nose and went down for the 'gravy'; my stomach felt wavy when I came back up for air, and puked over the side of the bed. We had that stink coming in at us all night as we hid under the bedclothes in fright and disgust, it certainly put paid to lust.

....
....

THE MIND STALKERS.
12/1/98

Whenever my ears burn with cold fire, I can't believe the nerve of whichever psychic pervert is picking up my thoughts via their ESP, and mulling over them and attempting to censure them and control me. It's left for hate and right for love, and I wish that by the stars above I could pinpoint these vile infiltrators and destroy them. Anyone who's never had their innermost private space violated, won't understand or believe what I'm trying to say; there are creatures out there that can literally prey upon your mind, they're the worst kind of devil spawn there is.

The callousness of these fiends can only be matched by mass murderers or contract killers; they have mounted a deliberate covert operation to try and drive me mad, as if my life isn't sad enough already. This monstrous perversion is known as 'long viewing' (and listening), the perpetrators have kept me stewing for years, impervious to my vitriolic castigations of their deeply underhand, cowardly tricks; use of the black arts is how they get their kicks. My harsh words of complaint can't touch that which has no soul. Mind stalkers are the aliens in our midst, monsters masquerading as humans, torturers into psychic S&M, warped telepaths, the evil undead with deadly intentions. But as with all predatory beasts, how do they protect themselves from their hunters? For there's no honour amongst ghouls, only fools could think they could trust anyone in their fraternity not to send them to an eternity of the damned. I've tried jamming my own airways, I've tried placing a lead-lined ring of steel around my mind, but they still find a way in and decipher, above all the din and torment therein, words that are relevant to them. And that's when they give your ears a tweak, causing you to back peddle to try and discern what meddlesome offence has been taken. It's a mind game of perilous proportions, against which I know of no precautions that work, amulets and crosses can't keep them out; it's the stuff that paranoid schizophrenia is made of; for after all, it's all in your head, nothing can be proved. Your enemies can smugly shrug and sympathetically imply that you're mad. I give back as good as I get, I'm mentally too strong for them, I taunt them to come crawling out of the ether and show themselves so I can give them a damned good hiding, but sneeringly they're biding their time till I'm near my death; and then they're going to come rushing at me with their fiendish faces glowing, and hiss in a knowing, echoing tone, "We know where you're going and about time too, all your life we've been trying to get rid of you, you should have died years ago, you pathetic mess. God knows we did our best to make you jump off that ledge, but you had to stick it out to this lonely, bitter end. What have you got to say to that...friend"? But it will be too late, I'll have already slipped into the tunnel of love that awaits all right-minded people, and I'll be hearing the bells from that heavenly steeple, and all my ills and cares will drop off me like the ticks they are. I'll get to occupy the star that has my name on it, bought and paid for while I served my time on Earth, and now the sole occupant of a dead world. And if my mind stalkers want to follow me there, they're welcome to whatever lean pickings they can find, because I reckon I'll be deaf, dumb and blind from sheer boredom. (I've signed off as 'the esteemed' Phil Fletcher on the original MS, wherever that is now. [Did I ever even write it?])

....

JAZZ ON A SUNDAY AFTERNOON.
15/6/98

At our local Trades Club, they have Jazz on a Sunday afternoon; it doesn't pay to go there too soon if, like me, you're always on your own, unless you like sitting alone. I used to go just to break up the day, put a few pints away, come home and crash out; I couldn't really understand what it was all about, this running up and down the scales with a laid back air, and quite frankly I didn't care. I've never understood chess either.
The slow stuff used to depress me, Sunday afternoons are bad enough; I dug it the most (can you still say that and get away with it?) when it went up tempo, bordering on a rough and tumble between various members of the band. The faster and harder it got, the nearer I was to the promised land of the cerebral orgasm; if I nearly had a heart spasm then they'd hit the spot for me. I usually sit at the bar on a rickety stool, I'm much too 'complexed' to sit staring reverently at the band, and anyway I can't make them out from where I'm sat, my eyesight isn't exactly where it's at when it comes to long distance vision. It's a bit of a mission impossible for me to make them out in the murky

light, I just try and give the impression I can see them when I turn precariously round after each casually structured set piece, to clap appreciatively.

But Sunday afternoon isn't Saturday night, and somehow the atmosphere never seemed right. Now that I'm too old to rock and can only mock those who are still 'mad for it', I like the idea of a cool, sultry atmosphere with nothing more to fear than a hung over Sunday morning; where the club has a sign that reads, 'LET ALL WHO ENTER IN HERE BE PREPARED TO DRINK BEER WITH WHISKY CHASERS, SPOTLIGHTS WILL CUT THROUGH THE SMOKE LIKE A KNIFE, YOU'LL BE IN A '50s TIMEWARP WHERE YOUR LIFE COULD BE IN DANGER FROM CHOKING ON THE FUMES OF REEFERS AND CIGARS. WHEN YOU COME OUT YOU'LL BE SHOOTING AT THE STARS WITH YOUR LASER PEN, AND WILL DEFINITELY WANT TO COME BACK HERE AGAIN NEXT WEEK'.
I wish I'd been a beatnik when The Jerry Mulligan Quartet sound was around, clicking my fingers in the school of cool, posing on the edge of the pool, and never getting my poetry wet from too much exposure. A jazz aficionado is something I'm not; to me it's either lukewarm or hot. I love it when there's steam coming out of the 'bull' sax player's ears, and the bass is so strong it has glasses jumping round the room; or else when a torch singer's crooning into the gloom about 'one for my baby and one more for the road', and at quarter to

three in the morning you can still get one, a drink that is, 'babies' are impossible to find when you're 51 and three parts blind.
(PLF. I entered the above for a projected anthology of jazz poetry, the originators eventually sent it back; the project had been cancelled. Was this their polite way of saying, "We don't want your largely depressing entry"? I, nor you, will never know. The next two pieces are copies of letters I sent, accompanying work, to firstly: 'BLOODAXE BOOKS', and later that same year, 1998, 'THE CARCANET PRESS'. I was rejected by both publishers; there are times when I think I'm not fit to be published, even in the most dismal of anthologies, but fortunately these moods pass. 13/6/02)

....

Dear BLOODAXE BOOKS, 4/1/98.

I read a review in a recent copy of The Writer's Year Book ('95), which stated that you are conceivably this country's biggest and best publishers of poetry today; he was published by you. So I thought I'd risk putting my fragile ego in your hands by enclosing for your perusal, and much hoped for approval, a few samples of my latest work. I call my type of poetry 'statements in rhyme', which, if I ever get into print, will be the title of my first 'slim vol', (not true, as it

subsequently turned out, 30/6/06). I've researched a lot of poetry over the years, and consider it to be a load of esoteric claptrap, and not a patch on mine, (delusions of grandeur? I got 'em.)
I wouldn't give you tuppence for Eliot's 'FOUR QUARTETS', and 'WASTELAND', especially after seeing that recent docu-drama which showed how badly he treated his wife; admirably played by Miranda Richardson. Sylvia Plath's later work is chillingly good, but I think you've had to be clinically depressed, (like what I've been, how's that for bad grammar?) to really appreciate it. I'd like to be on a par with John Cooper Clarke, or 'The million pound poet' (who's now disappeared off the scene as meteorically fast as he came onto it), and actually make some money out of my talent; and with 'new labour' threatening to reduce benefits for disabled people, I might be forced to…or starve.
I'm nearly 51 years old, I've been visually handicapped all my life, and now I have Arthritis and Spondulitis, (that last one sounds like something THE GOONS could have come up with.) If I ever get accepted by anyone, I've got my own artwork for the cover of my volume; it's very eye-catching and accessible, which is what I believe modern poetry should be. You can keep all your cryptic stuff for your highbrow intellectuals, who're too mean to buy books anyway, except from musty-smelling charity shops. I don't know what I'll do if you turn me down, I've set my heart on being published by you, I like your name and

you're not as far away as London; I'll just have to go back to being a sad old git if you won't have me, I'll probably get clinically depressed again. Yours, etc. (How could they have refused me after a letter like that? I ask you?)

....

Dear CARCANET PRESS, 28/8/98,

my name is Phil Fletcher, I'm 51 years old, I've been attempting to become a writer for the last 25 years. I've had a few poems accepted by magazines, nothing worth shouting about, and I have an entry in this year's ARVON poetry comp', which might well sink without trace along with its predecessors. Being a mad impetuous fool, I've decided to send you copies of my three latest creations, I have stacks of completed work should you be remotely interested in my somewhat unorthodox style.
I believe that writing is a contract between the author and his/her potential readers, as long as there's a warning on the coveted book cover stating that the book contains explicit material, then no-one should complain that their senses have been shocked without prior notice. I think all I do is reflect the truth the way a lot of my generation view it; even if you are over subscribed with poets hoping to hit the big time, and have no choice

other than to reluctantly return my work, could you please offer me a few words of encouragement and reassure me that my genius will be recognised one day? And finally, if all else fails will you kindly let me know what CARCANET means? It's really infuriating when you can't find a word in The Oxford English Dictionary.

Yours with a sense of trepidation, yet at the same time tinged with a hint of facetiousness, which I'm trying unsuccessfully to cure myself of.
PS, I've decided to throw in an earlier example of my work as well. Mr Philip Louis Fletcher.
(My efforts were returned, along with the dreaded 'Dear unsuccessful one' slip.)

....
....

CRACK.   22/8/98

Crack cocaine coursing through my brain like a shot of electro-convulsive treatment, jolting me into an acute state of mental activity, helping me to understand Einstein's theory of relativity and improve upon it, before I forget, and come out of this delirious trance all clammy and wet, like an unwiped bum crack.
Actually, I've never taken the stuff, microdot LSD was enough for me, back in 1970; and for a few

years beyond. It was a really amazing chemical, you could hardly see it in the palm of your hand, but if you swallowed it, it was your passport to an adult version of Alice Cooper in Wonderland for, 10 or 12 hours, such magical powers contained in something so small. You'd go into freefall and when you stabilised you'd be surprised at everything around you, it would all seem so new and clearly defined in a child-like way.

Your ever-expanding mind could cope for a time before panic set in, "Am I going to be in this naive and vulnerable state for all time? And what is the real time? I keep forgetting. I can only distinguish between dark and light, it could be darkness at noon for all I know, or an eclipse of the moon and sun. I might fly out the window of my mind's eye to spy on the universe and see if I can't put time in reverse, and have a word with 'GOD' about how can 'he' be such a callous sod to let this, his Crown of Creation, be left in the hands of fools, who've shattered all the rules of common, global decency".

....
......

LIVING WITHOUT SOCIAL AND EMOTIONAL IMPROVEMENT.

(i swear the critics will never get me.)
15/8/98

I'm forced to alter my emotions along with the changing of the seasons; I don't want to, I'd prefer to stay the same way, like an endless summer's day. I don't relish the prospect of feeling compulsively wistful as the mists of autumn come drifting in, I'd rather be wallowing in the sin of a purloined sexual endeavour, like the seduction of a 16-year-old nun, just for fun.
But then I'd feel a pang of wintry remorse that I'd turned this sweet butterfly into a rocking horse for my own pointless, lust-driven exertions. These kind of coercions are best found in 'wank mags' only; though there are plenty who wouldn't need much persuading that such delicious young fruit is best plucked from the vine early before it becomes overripe and fly-blown.
They either hunt alone or in packs, wearing uniforms; atrocities are the norm when a war's been declared, each side out-daring the other in acts of violation of human rights. Perhaps it's only fear of moral censorship that's making me adopt such a socially responsible line; after all, I've got very little to thank women for, (not even my deceased mother), and a lot of reasons to hate them. Not too long ago, I saw one interviewed on TV who'd voluntarily had sex with 251 men in a space of ten hours, using condoms of course, just to prove the point that she could if she wanted to. (Annabel Chong.)

Yet the same woman could have a man charged with rape if she woke up next to him after going home with him, 'rat arsed', and not remembering his face in the cold light of day. She could have him put away or seriously inconvenienced, lenience wouldn't be in her vocabulary if she thought he'd taken something without her consent; even if he was on 'the vinegar strokes' and she changed her mind, she could drag him through the unholy grind of our blind idiot legal system, if he couldn't pull out in time, and not spill his slimy mess on the hem of her dress.
All in all, this nightmare stress of sexual inequality is enough to take the spring out the step of any full-blooded male, my sperm's grown stale through a lack of release into its preferred orifice.

....

DOPE.
21/8/98

Lost all hope? Use dope. Have a pronounced death wish? Inject heroin and leave your works in a dirty dish by your grubby mattress on the floor, always expecting your door to be kicked in by the law looking for more 'stash' than you could ever afford to buy from the stuff you steal. You could always deal or be a courier, but you're too much of a worrier to carry either dubious occupation off with suitable aplomb. Alcohol's the easiest and cheapest way to go 'down below', with white cider at two pounds a throw for a large flagon, you could keep yourself groggy all day, with half an ounce of rolling tobacco to emphasise your lordly state; and when you start to hate everything and everyone you meet, and you can't take the heat of a constant diet of alcohol and smoke any longer, if you're lucky you can go to a place where people are a lot stronger than you, who'll know what to do about your immediate state of rabid hate for life.

They won't use a knife to cut the poison out, they'll hit you with a chemical cosh instead, keeping you tied to your bed with your limbs feeling like lead and your head blown up like a balloon filled with methane gas, you'll be talking out your 'ass' for some little time to come.

....
....

PLUGGED IN.
14/9/98

One of the things I most like to see is a black-coated plug in its socket, feeding electricity into my portable hi fi system, out of which I can record for free my favourite sounds on a 90 minute cassette tape (it was 1998). I'm agape with awe at this positive combination of science and technology, if it was left to my inventive powers we'd still be rubbing two sticks together for hours just to get a spark; in fact I doubt if I could have invented that! I'd have gone to bed when it got dark, and got up again to wash myself in the rain, and have a good scratch and wonder who I could coax to sew a patch on my loin cloth to keep my balls from hanging out.

At the first signs of a food shortage, I'd have been knocked on the head, it being realised I was dead from the neck up when it came to serving a useful purpose to the tribe; except to eat more than my fair share of the fare gathered and brought in by the rest, thus fattening myself up for this supreme sacrifice. I'd want to taste nice and juicy for them and be remembered with a good belch and a fart. The worst use of electricity I can think of is the electric chair. Anyone who's had a mild electric shock will know what an ugly, devilish sensation it is. Imagine the terror of being strapped in that chair and then connected to the mains, knowing your brains were going to be literally fried!? It would be better to have died a death inflicted by a thousand cuts...but not much better...but me no buts.

....

NOWHERE TO RUN, NOWHERE TO GO.
2/10/98

I'm lying in bed in the murky half light of another grey morning, listening to RADIO 3, manna from heaven to a soul hungry for the fulfilling effect classical music can have on it at this relatively early hour of the day; it's coming up to 7am. Immediately after the gloomy 3-minute news bulletin, there's an impressive rendition of Bach's lovely third partite in D, played on an eight-stringed guitar by a man whose name I can't remember; I snuggle deeper under my duvet in the warmth of my appreciation.
At 7.45am, the pleasant female announcer announces in her not unpleasant Irish accent, that we are now going to hear an unusual version of Ravel's 'MOTHER GOOSE SUITE'; I love Ravel. As I lie there in enraptured anticipation, a sudden rainsquall begins lashing at my nice, not very big, double-glazed bedroom window; as well as drumming on the roof. This was perfect, what more could a man alone in bed ask for? I was snug and warm, the sound of the rain was blending in with music by one of my favourite composers?
It was while enjoying this idyllic interlude of peace and harmony that the thought came into my mind along the lines of, "Why does the world outside

have to be so awfully aggressive"? My nerves are already in shreds from all the ugly mechanical noise that I have to endure from the busy A646 nearby, and now, in the little side street that my kitchen windows face onto, I've got a clown who loves to park his high-powered, murdering wheelchair, (a car to him) right opposite them. Not only that, as if this wasn't bad enough, lately he's been causing horrendous noise pollution from its clapped-out exhaust. This is red rag to a bull and I've been giving him the V sign through the window and yelling obscenities at him. Now I'm living in fear of getting my head kicked in for showing the moron disrespect; 'THE MOTHER GOOSE SUITE' finishes to rapturous applause from the raindrops.

8 o'clock, there's no point in my getting up before 9am. If it weren't for daytime telly, there'd be no point in my getting up much before midday; in my opinion anyway. I could really enjoy my low-key, low budget existence if I could keep the hideously frenetic, modern world at bay. I love radio and TV; they've helped me to complete my education since leaving school at fifteen, 36 years ago.

But of course, I'm not contributing anything towards society, I'm a drain on the public purse, (a bit like the duke and duchess of Kent), and the tax paying 'locals' resent this, and that's why they go out of their way to make life uncomfortable for me; or so my paranoia keeps telling me.

At 8.30am, the car user from hell's engine roars into life, right through my solid stone walls and into my sanctuary. I'm instantly traumatised and out of bed, stark naked, rushing to the second floor window of my monk's closet to see if I can spot him hurtling round the corner on two wheels; I cup my manhood in one hand. Too late, I've missed the bastard; I need to know for certain it's him before I can complain to the police.

I now realise that the whole neighbourhood has clocked this naked pervert exposing himself to all and sundry; and those who haven't witnessed this terrible spectacle directly, will soon be informed in lurid details. It's 8.35 am now, and I've crawled back into bed feeling totally sensitised. I feel as though I've suffered an electric shock. If only there was somewhere I could run to, to escape this daily grind of persecution; just me and my radio, TV, and CD collection, in a haven of peace and tranquillity; there's a youth hostel at Mankinholes I could check out, but I doubt if they'd let me live there permanently. (As well as a Buddhist monastry...not at Mankinholes.)

The planet's already seemingly in terminal decline from too much global conspicuous consumption, the total human population explosion is accelerating out of control, it's expected to reach 6 billion before the year 2000. Why won't people slow down? After all, death is Nature's way of telling you to. We've become like the proverbial lemming, with a strong hint of head-burying ostrich thrown in; we choose to ignore the signals of global warming, (not necessarily happening here, but everywhere else), holes in the ozone

layer, rapid denuding of the Earth's resources........etc.
Maybe I should go forth with a 'YOU'RE ALL DOOMED' placard on my back, and a begging bowl for alms, to preach to the multitudes before it's too late; or maybe I should have another hour in bed instead?

....

REJECTION...FOR MEN.
15/9/98

How much rejection should it take before your spirit breaks and you want to lay down and die? Big bad boring death, there will go I when I've been separated from my breath. Now I know for certain that Hell IS other people; like the growing numbers of other 'singles', I'm not sorry that I live alone. But I still need that 'Special one' to help me in my 'me against the world' existence, though the ones I've met have been femininely
disguised 'HELL'S ANGELS', with hearts as black as the blackest holes; they've had the looks, but sold their souls to become control freaks.
They want to control and dominate 'their man' in bed, and have him fuck them till he's nearly dead; and if he can't do 'the business' on demand, they'll take their ever open sore and offer it to anyone

who takes their fancy. I flicked on to CHANNEL 4 late the other night and gave my senses an awful fright; there was a woman fucking a man up the arse with a dildo on!! That saw my last vestige of hope in humanity gone; if you have to be that disaffected to 'get it on', what would you be willing to do if you were feeling really frustrated? Have the whole male race castrated after being 'milked', then gassed and burnt, and have males only born 'to order' in your rampant, rapacious, lesbian world? Deadlier than the male in intent, if unrestrictedly allowed to have their head, (a Freudian slip there). Historically it's been proven that women need to be kept under control, they think they can rule the world with their holes; they know a man's weakness is in his cock, and they use his lack of (potential) 'staying up' power to mock and shame him; to defame him in front of his friends; their sexual rapaciousness never ends.
24/10/98
To fall in love is a curse, because if it turns out she's shagging half the street while you're out at work, there's no worse pain you can endure. And if you kill her for her infidelity, you'll pay a penalty that's hard to bear; banged up in a total male ATMOSFEAR! Where men don't use dildos to fuck each other up the arse, and the milk of human kindness is very sparse indeed. I guess I'll just remain at home alone, a one-eyed King on his lonely throne, nipping out only to pick up supplies from the shops.

And if one day they break in and find me, six months after I've been dead, with a crown of scabs around my rotted head, and a final death's grimace on my emaciated face, they'll be welcome to plunder all my possessions that gave my life so much grace; books, records, tapes, CDs and videos by the score, my vicarious gratifications no use to me any more.
(My last poem?) (Obviously not. 17/6/02)

....

I WANT A 'FARTING' FANNY FOR CHRISTMAS. 29-30/10/98

I've never heard a 'farting' fanny, or enjoyed the pleasures of a '69er', my sex life is less active than that of a well rotted corpse, who possibly had sex on the brain when it was plucked untimely from thinking about sex. I've got a hex on me as far as love and lust fulfilment are concerned, all I've ever got is my ego and libido burned...and spurned! I only learned about the farting fanny from reading the problem page in women's mag's, and I wouldn't want a 69er if the woman was on her 'rags'.
The sex industry is fraught with snags if you're an unwary punter, it can cost you your job if you're a

high-class 'hunter' and pick the wrong prey. It can cost you your life if you're not prepared to pay enough care to prevent Nature's more deadly marauders infiltrating and destroying your natural defences. Still, it's hard to retain your senses if you get it offered to you on a plate, and it's too late to go and buy a packet of 'MATES'. If you're like me, it might be worth your while to cop for a deadly dose, dying slowly and tragically might give me time to rekindle my faith in the holy grail and the holy ghost, and ponder upon the exact location of heaven.

During sex is the only time two people really (or do I mean rarely?) come together; after all they're both in search of a common goal, the cock and the cunt fusing in orgasm. I might as well be blunt; if you're in love it's even better, hotter and wetter than your mates brag about down at the pub. Masturbation is for sad old gits who can't get arrested, I've already invested in my own wanking chariot; and I've bought a 'blow-up' doll called Charlotte; I wonder if I can get her fanny to fart for me? I'll have to see, the next time I'm feeling frisky on a Saturday night. At least 'C' won't get so excited she'll be in danger of losing control of her bowels at the moment of bliss; I'll be able to deflate her ardour with a hiss of satisfaction. I hope your reactions won't be too judgmental about what I get up to in my lonely state; it's bad enough that myself I hate.

If I can't be found worthy enough of a 'soul' and shagging mate, what am I supposed to do? Come round and watch you do the business 3 times nightly? Or step lightly past parked cars down lovers' lane? None of it's worth the pain of a broken heart, I find it impossible to find a 'tart' in this blatantly promiscuous age; from what I've heard most of them only want your money anyway, and not your sex. What an awful job to do if you don't enjoy it, it's a high risk career and no mistake; as a moneymaking venture I wouldn't employ it, unless I was a really hard-nosed pimp, who wouldn't skimp on a physical warning if my 'girls' didn't bring home loads of cash in the morning.

....

MINIMALISM. "My life's worth fuck-all". "Is that it"? "Yep"! 9/12/98.

....

WILD SKY IN MY EYE. (ONLY THE SKY IS TRULY FREE.)
(Begun 5/11/98, finished 27/11/98.)

The sky lives on forever, and when I die I want to capture an image of it, the wilder and more extravagant the better. Windier and wetter than I've ever seen it before, with the lightning as bright as a thousand suns, and the thunder so loud it will echo for evermore.

Life is just an interruption of the void that existed before your birth, and which will continue after you cease to be; unless you opt for immortality like Frankenstein's monster, (not the Boris Karlof model I hasten to add.))

If, at the point of death, I found myself chained to the main mast of an eighteenth century sailing ship, like the painter William Turner used to do in order to feel and observe the fullest effects of sea storms, and one of these cataclysmic events was ongoing, I might make a Faustian appeal to the elements to give me eternal life so I could ride high in the sky on the backs of clouds. Or curl up at night beneath the stars on the side of the cumulous mountains, looking down at the gleaming specks of car headlights and wrinkling my nose up at the reek of their exhaust fumes. And when I'd had enough of that depressing sport I'd cavort across an ocean, riding the waves, leaping from one moonlit breaker to the next, to land eventually on a virgin shore.

And once there I could dance on the beach to the music of the spheres, the sun, the moon, the stars, and this heady mixture would be as tantalising as the song of the Sirens in my ears. And if I grew lonely, I would fashion an Eve from the grains of sand that abounded, only waiting to be brought to life; I could even build a castle for us to live in and have coffee-coloured children by the score. And if marauding pirates ever came too near, I would shatter their illusions of my reality by obliterating what I had created with my own pair of hands. What no other man but me had torn asunder, I could rebuild at my leisure, measure for measure, always sculpting different beautiful faces to take the place of those whose disintegrated fragments had been carried off on the coastal winds and waters, to every nook and cranny of the globe. My renewable family would have voices, with voice textures that could mimic Nature's creatures, the seagull for the harpy and the harridan, the dolphin for the precocious brat, and the humpbacked whale for the lonely and the lovelorn. Oh, and the seal pup crying like a new born baby, alerting the hunter to come and stove its head in so he could steal its skin to wrap *his* baby bunting in. On certain nights, I'll be able to ride on the back of the gibbous moon as if she were a great white porpoise, ploughing through the luminous silver clouds; disappearing and reappearing as the swell takes us; and if I want a glimpse into hell I can look down into the well of an active volcano, and from my omnipotent vantage point on its fiery rim, I'd demand that the uneducated mass of humanity be hurled in; the only way their collective sin of ignorance can be expunged, to be cleansed by fire. Only then will my ire, brought on by their unrelenting crimes against the rest of the planet's ecology, be assuaged. Enraged as I am towards all negativity, I know it's in me to rest idly on my

laurels and say "FUCK OFF"! to all morals and their restricting consequences, 'Do what thou wilt', has always been the whole of the law in the hands of mono, and megalomaniacs galore; not any more, or for too much longer anyway; not if I have my say with the Gods on their Olympian heights. "Twat 'em big style in your holy war against their effrontery upon your wondrous creations, no more close relations with humanoids, they've left massive voids where other flora and fauna used to be".
But all too soon, misery comes to haunt me, as I look out my window on one more murky grey day, my life is just time passing, and all my aspirations come to nought; my mood is as decayed as the smell of the body gas that escapes from me. The older I get, existence seems more like playing Russian roulette; I go to sleep never knowing if I'm going to wake up again...
(Is this my magnum exodus?)

....

SUMP. (FOR THE LACK OF THE LOVE OF A GOOD-LOOKING WOMAN.) 1/12/98

Getting drunk's okay, you can drink your troubles away without having to pay a fortune; if it's merely the alcohol you're after. I like the sound of my own laughter as I sink into my cups; for all too brief a moment all my downs feel like ups. "Fuck 'em all", I hear myself say, "they're all a pile of shite"! And then I curse them inside my head with all my drunken might.

If they won't accept and return my love, they can incur my wrath and suffer the consequential blight... "AND IF THEY WANT A FIGHT THEY CAN FUCKING WELL HAVE ONE"!

I don't go out anymore, there's nothing to entice me out the door; I'm much too old for the cesspit that is 'club land', the human animal at its predatory worst. I sit in front of my TV and quench my thirst to feel a part of a great, invisible plan; not just one more lonely and disillusioned man wrecking what's left of his health, getting pissed by himself in the hope that he'll never wake up again.

There's a deliciousness in the pain of self pity that can only be felt when you're three parts sloshed, it gives you the incentive to go all the way to drunken oblivion; no-one cares any way. So you cram another can of 9% alcohol down your neck, and inhale deeply a few more cigarettes; blinking and gasping at the TV until you see two sets, and you're bored out of your skull to such an extent that to sit up for one more minute would be more than you could bear, you slope off to bed and are glad to be going there.

I know when I've had the right amount before I slump into a stupor, out for the count; I'll lie there with my mind a blank, feeling like an innocent child. If the Neil Gaiman image of DEATH came to collect me now, I'd greet her with a beatific smile and ask her if there was any chance of a shag before she led me away? I'm sure she'd understand, if not actually oblige. Her manner is so open and reassuring, I'd follow her anywhere, anyhow; not like her sister 'DESPAIR', a hideously fat and ugly sow, enough to sober anyone up...in a hurry!

(To the uninitiated, Neil Gaiman is the creator of 'SANDMAN'.)
MADNESS. (THE REAL MEANING OF WORDS.) 1/12/98

'Turd', is a word that you wouldn't necessarily associate with a piece of shit; it rhymes with 'Richard the Third' and sometimes the aforementioned piece of shit is called a 'richard'. "Insane shit-stains", is a derogatory name I have for the marauding maggoty scum that are my own personal 'mind-stalkers'. Like shadows, deep black and dense, silently screaming, pawing at my grave for a ghoulish feast, is how I feel when I detect them sucking at my life's blood; I must have done something good in a previous life to deserve the strife these undead creatures cause me. Madness is a state of mind most commonly observed in humankind; other species have eccentric traits, like dolphins regarding humans as mates. Or whales not having enough sense to dive down deep and keep themselves there for as long as they can, as soon as the killing ships from Norway and Japan draw near; maybe they think they look too small to fear.

Rabies is probably the worst form of madness, once it sets in there's no known cure, it's the ultimate in DNA designer horror; you'd be better off being shot like a mad dog or a boar. It destroys your soul before it kills you, your death you will implore to come and relieve you, as the terror inside you grows more and more. (Scary stuff, I wonder if mosquitoes can spread rabies from drinking the blood of infected victims? Just in case I get stung in Thailand sometime? 30/6/06.)

....

TRYING TO UNWIND THE DARK SIDE OF THE HUMAN MIND.
10/2/99.

It's not a straightforward case of good versus evil we have here, sometimes there's complicity on both sides, adding to the fear of insanity. And insanity unchecked is a downward spiral into Hell! Some of us are born victims of our psyches, our egos too close to the id, primeval echoes come back to haunt us, black thoughts jump out unbid. A large minority aren't afraid of their dark side, they embrace it as the norm, the threat of being caught and caged doesn't constrain them; they're evil incarnate in human form.

Some of them have committed mass murder, seemingly without any regret, behind the guise of a military uniform. One notorious Second World War criminal admitted publicly, recently, that he was only following orders; but privately I think he was having fun with a gun. He said on TV: "You just put the pistol to the back of their heads, pulled the trigger, they fell down and that was it", but were all his victims instantly dead, or dying horribly, slowly?

The catalogue of diabolical cruelty and destruction is endless, and stretches right back to the dawn of human history, though what provokes it appears to be an unsolvable mystery. Hatred and prejudice are in our genes, I know they're in mine; but I'd draw the line at physically acting upon my prejudice and hate-driven fantasies, except perhaps against myself when all my orifices become too much of a nuisance to bear, and I no longer care to mop up after their emissions, and my limbs and lungs aren't much stronger than those of a 12-month-old child, and my thoughts are so mild they don't even cause a ripple.

....……..

THE NEW NILLENNIUM.
23/3/99.

Greet the new Nillennium, it's the same as the old one except that now we've got the Internet, and you're totally wet unless you're online all the time. And we've got a clapped-out cabaret artist being paid a fortune (ten million dollars) to whip up hysteria on the eve of the new era, as queerer and queerer become the norm. If I was the Avenging Angel and it was Judgement Day, I'd blow that ageing singer away straightaway, using the latest ray gun technology; for anyone to delude themselves that she's worth a fraction of what she's being paid, defies all transubstantiationalist belief.
In fact, if I were the avenging angel, I wouldn't wait till Judgement day, I'd ZAP! everyone on my hate list right now, my irritability level's gone so high. I wouldn't even bother to whisper, 'Your end is nigh', just WHAP! 'em right thru' the eyes with my high-powered laser, or viciously stab a toxic finger into their heads.
I sometimes envisage a labyrinth of emptiness and dread, harbouring Absolute Evil at its magnetic core, total nihilism as depicted in the infamous painting by Goya of Saturn devouring one of his offspring. Perhaps I would behave like him in my role of The Avenging Angel of Death to obscenely overpaid cabaret singers.

....

IS ONANISM THE SAME AS SOLIPSISM? (Or: HEDONISM DOESN'T PAY.)
Both young, and old men and women, indulge in onanism and solipsism, usually from force of circumstance; nobody understands them, or they're dismissed at a glance. Some people are born onanists, others have onanism forced upon them; nobody wants to fuck, or be fucked by them, unless it's a very dark night and they're pissed and the offending disgrace to the human race isn't still hanging round in the morning, hoping for a second helping.
I am a wanking solipsist, (more infrequently on the bishop-bashing front now I'm getting older), it helps me to get to sleep on those soulless nights when the physical need for sexual release is pulsating through my genitalia; the potential makings of another life are wiped off my belly indifferently, who would want to inflict another ME on the world? Certainly not me.
I'm existing in a vacuum, nothing gets in and nothing escapes; except perhaps my instinct for self preservation. I'm a rocky outcrop in a hostile

and malevolent sea, at times I wish its waves would wash over me and put me out of my misery. The most positive charge to be made about onanism is that in your hand your penis feels really large, and you can indulge in lewd, lascivious, and fantastic acts with someone who, in the flesh, wouldn't touch you with a ten-foot barge pole; and you usually drop off to sleep shortly after you've 'chucked your muck'. Not as far as I could wish any more, though at the point of no return it feels like a geyser about to blow, it's very rare for my leading Kami kasi pilot sperm to crash-land anywhere higher than my navel; still, if it was doing the job it was intended for, that would be far enough if my cock had been beavering away inside a hairy muff.

If there was a way that fate could repay me for all the spiritual malnutrition I've had to suffer in my time on Earth, it would be to grant me a rebirth in the after life, where I'd drink and smoke all day and night if I wanted to, with no fearful comedown to dread...I'll already be dead. And if I had to stay me, could I go back to being 23 with a nose job and glasses-free, and my long lustrous hair and greatcoat back, and a rucksack to carry my heavenly stash in, a 'MR TAMBOURINE MAN' for eternity. (Can I substitute the tambourine for an acoustic guitar and 'harp'?). Where all the beautiful and enigmatic women couldn't resist following me into that jingle jangle morning, not at the same time but individually. And after we'd had our magical affair, I wouldn't be there for

them, I'd already be up and gone, dueting with the blackbird and the robin on my penny whistle or pan pipes.
And I'd never grow cynical or jaded, or faded. Each time I found the crock of gold at the end of a rainbow I'd be re-energised to go and sew my wild oats again and again...and again....and again .....and again......!
(This epic, begun on the 11/4/99, wasn't completed till 5/6/99.)

....

THE TUNNEL OF LOVE. Or: COPING WITH MADNESS. 24/1/99

A beautiful suggestion was put to me, but I was too drunk to deal with it properly, I don't think it will ever be put to me again.

....

THE SIMPLE LIFE.   24/1/99

My mind can't cope with complications, it's a type of dyslexia that I suffer from, deeper than nothingness, darker than despair.

(PS. 10/6/99. I've now joined The Hourglass Writers in Hebden Bridge, thus affording myself a new lease of life, not much else has changed. (20/6/02, That avenue of escape from literary and social isolation has now more or less fizzled out due to too many unbridgeable differences between various members of the group.)

....……

THE GREAT ACHE. (Easter Sunday. 5/4/99.)

'SITTIN' ON THE DOCK OF THE BAY', sums up my life. The words: 'And this loneliness won't leave me alone', defines the internal strife I suffer as a consequence of this barren state; totally alone, victim of a sadistic and schizoid fate. Example: 52 years old, no wife, no kids, no luck, no friends, no social life to speak of.

....…..

MANIFEST HEAVEN, RIGHT HERE ON EARTH.   3/5/99

Anne Sophie Mutter isn't a name that exactly trips off my tongue, unlike 'Sophie Tucker', last of the red-hot mommas. Indeed, I'd never heard of Anne Sophie Mutter till the middle of last week when she turned up on BBC2 at 11.20pm in a programme off-puttingly titled: 'My Year With Beethoven', which I tuned into halfway through because there was nothing else worth watching on my choice-limiting four terrestrial channels.
And what an astonishing surprise I had, there was this beautiful young woman looking straight along her violin at me with a look of rapt concentration on her face. I was amazed when the camera panned out, it revealed a stunning off-the-shoulder, full length, two-toned blue dress, and she was standing tall in it, head and shoulders above her piano playing accomplice; a non descript looking man with a nearly bald head.
A Beethoven violin sonata has never sounded so good to me before, or its performer seemed so enchanting, I normally find watching classical music being performed a big turnoff. What a glowing example of manifest destiny she is, young, beautiful, a naturally gifted, highly intelligent woman; she'd be so nice for me to come home to after a hard day at the betting shop and the pub; especially if she had an intellectually designed supper laid on, and her violin out ready to soothe my aching brow and sore head, with the possibility

of a passionate night's dueting ahead, and never a cross word about my constant drain on her financial resources.

On the other hand, a glaring example of manifest destiny was displayed in Channel 4's new series about self-build homes, called 'GRAND DESIGNS'. This quintessential, politically correct (Tony Blair would be proud of them) English family, Mr and Mrs 'To those that hath shall be given' and their five lovely children; they've even gallingly named their latest arrival 'Tiger', which is a hard name to live up to, the boy might turn out to be more of a 'Tigger', and a sensitive soul like me.

This was another programme I turned on halfway through, after watching the compulsive 'Animal Hospital'; I wish some creature would seriously bite Rolf Harris on screen so he'd be actually forced to climb that 'STAIRWAY TO HEAVEN' (his version of the Led Zeppelin 'classic') that he's done his best to destroy during his time on Earth. My envious hackles rose as soon as I realised I was watching people who have everything I haven't, their whinging on about minor hiccups with the builders had me sneering in my old rocking chair in my cramped and claustrophobic little house; "Manifest destiny", I snarled, "manifest fucking destiny"!

Even though they've gone dangerously over budget without managing to be repossessed, and survived the agonies of moving into their palatial 'des res', (they've got gold leaf in their kitchen!),

they're able to cope and their new home is already worth £30,000 more than it cost them to build. If they're not the pride of 'cool' Britannia, I don't know who is? Not me that's for sure.
I'M SO HAPPY, HA, HA, HA! (SICK LAUGHTER.) 9/5/99

I recently learned that the fundamental teaching of Buddhism is that the root of all human suffering is desire. After some serious consideration, I've come to the conclusion that there's nothing wrong in desiring a healthy dose of fame, fortune and romance, it's only suffering and torture if your desires remain unfulfilled. If I gave up on desire I'd give up on getting out of bed in the mornings, or early afternoons, and I'd soon starve to death doing that, as I'm too young to qualify for meals on wheels, and care in the community won't stretch to do itemised shopping for the single man, or wiping his backside.
I think it's a basic instinct for every creature to desire what's best for itself, that's why in Nature, only the fittest survive. The programme that pointed out to me the first principle of Buddhism was about the biggest Buddhist temple ever built in the world, in Java; which had lain hidden beneath volcanic debris and tropical growth for nearly a thousand years.
If my garbled memory serves me well, and it doesn't usually, novice Buddhist monks had to pass through seven stages of enlightenment before they could gain admittance to the highest level of

the temple; by which time they were so enlightened they would literally float off into the ether in a cross-legged trance to 'The Inn Of The Seventh Happiness', next door to 'The House Of The Rising Sun', just a little way from the pagoda on top of the 'Mountains of The Moon'.

A strong compulsion I have to avoid now, unless I want to 'Break On Through To The Other Side', like my ultimate rock hero Jim Morrison, is to seek enlightenment and oblivion through alcohol and mind expanding drugs; there might well be nothing on the other side except an army of lost souls who crossed over too soon; chief among them Jim Morrison and Jimi Hendrix. Youth is indeed wasted on the young, and if they die too soon through unwise over-indulgence, they'll certainly find that Hell is full of people who were too fast to live, like themselves.

I think it's tragic that so many young people are giving up on life before they've even found out what it's really all about, achieving personal fulfilment in a positive way; or at least not in a negatively destructive fashion. Unlike desire, I'm convinced that a sense of a lack of any real purpose or talent, and social isolation, are our two greatest forms of suffering, and our biggest killers. Both ailments have nearly finished me off at various times in this cut-and-thrust struggle for existence.

Even if you're content not to amount to anything very much, there are unseen pressures out there waiting to hound you out of your blissful state of complacency; such as the 'Welfare to Work' pogrom. So now I'm not so much trying to reinvent myself, as rebuild my health, in order to cheat the grim reaper for as long as possible; especially if he looks anything like the hooded horror who appeared in a crowded train compartment in a recent TV ad for life insurance. He was so gruesome-looking, he nearly frightened the life out of me; thankfully I'm already covered for the inevitable main event.

(The mind stalking evil ones are gnawing at my vitals today, it's been a struggle against an imposed sense of hopelessness to get this piece typed up; I've only got four poems left to transcribe, I hope the typewriter ribbon will hold out because then I'M FINISHED with writing!.....I mean it......I REALLY DO.!)   11/6/99

....

LONE SHARK.
20/5/99

The Sun, 93 million miles away and stone free,
Looked straight down at me as I lay basking in the nearly deserted

Park, like a lone shark. The first spark of summer warmth
Revitalised the skin on my face, making my surroundings feel a
Less lonely place than usual. But I mustn't lie there too long in case
Those invisible harmful rays give me fatal skin cancer later on.
5 more minutes and I'll be gone, slinking out like a guilty man
Past the happy, healthy family clan, playing on the swings and squealing down the slide. I try and hide my bulk as much as I can till
I'm safely by; I dread some infant shouting, "Who's that man mum"?
Or, "Why is he in the park? Parks are for families and children, why
Mam, why"?
"Because I don't have any garden", I'd sigh, "and on rare sunny
Days like these, it's nice to feel the breeze in your hair and the sun
On your face, and smell the fragrance of the sweet scented stock
In the borders, without being seen as one of that band of marauders
Who've made urban terrorism such a constant threat; like predators
On the hunt for sweet and succulent deer. But you needn't fear, I'm

More afraid of you than you could ever be of me; I want to remain free in body and in mind. If I ever find a peaceful haven, I'll leave this human Jungle safely behind me".

....

I WISH I HADN'T EATEN IT SO QUICKLY.   23/5/99

I've just eaten a mass produced quiche, filled with God alone
Knows what, but I don't care; I'd be a lot more hungry and depressed
If it hadn't been there in the fridge, waiting for me, already past its use by date.
It looked really big when I dumped it out onto the plate, should I eat half now and wait Till later to do justice to the rest, or do what I usually do, wolf it down and regret it at My leisure? I've got a bloated feeling inside my gut, I've stayed true to form; it seems I'm too old and greedy to reform; after all, you never really know where your next Meal's coming from in this precarious world, Mr Milosovic might decide to bomb Todmorden in a last ditch attempt to defy NATO.
I don't think there was any genetically modified potato (without an 'e') in that pie, not That I'll feel any effects if there were, for another 20 years or so. Oh well, we've all got To go sometime, and I'm past my prime now. I wish they could invent a

strain of food That stopped you feeling self conscious and afraid, and not caring if you ever got laid Again, or even paid again; except in happy 'lo-fat chips with everything'. I think I'd Become King of the lo-fat happy chip eaters, especially if I could have hypoallergenic Curry sauce on, and my mushy peas were organically produced, and my one cal diet Coke could give me a boost, like a rocket up my rear. I need never fear my insignificant And obscure fate any more, if I could fork and pour such futuristic fodder down my neck, a bushel and a peck at a time.

....

ODDMENTS.

Thank Nod for those vital hours of sleep that keep insanity at bay.
21/3/98

The 'squab' is watching and devouring me in my small corner,

A life of complete sobriety? NO WAY!

My life should have been so beautiful, born into the right society at the right time in history; my life should have been as sweet and fragrant as peaches, and as tangy as limes. Instead of which, it's smelled and tasted like shit, all because my ugly face doesn't fit into the beautiful people's scheme of things. Well that's okay, I can live with that, it's going without 'twat' that's the hardest part; it's made a shrivelled lump out of my heart. (Rubbish or what?)   12/5/98.

A 'squab' is a cross between a squatter and a grub, and I've got one 'squabbing' inside me, using me as its unwilling living host. (No date, sometime in '98.)

While I was alive I might have walked past people and they may have thought,'Who does that cocky bastard think he is'? Buskers for instance, I rarely gave.   19/11/98

Life just complicates the 'before and after' of your existence. 23/11/98

And now the older I get, going to sleep at night is like playing Russian roulette, I never know if I'm going to wake up again in the morning. 26/11/98.

....

I DYE MY HAIR.
18/5/99

If people think I'm vain or pathetic I don't care, I dye my hair.
If I could afford to, I'd have my teeth whitened, using the latest laser
Treatment, to match my thatch. At least it's not a wig, and my teeth aren't false Choppers; I could bite the noses off over-zealous shoppers
If they tried to beat me to the diamond studded thong counter at
Harrods in the event of a sale, or chew the ears off their owners if they'd got to the last Pail of instant tanning sludge before me.
I want women to adore me, as I grow older, not abhor me as I disappear beneath layer Upon layer of ever whitening grey; with only my DNA to identify who I used to be;
The ageing process won't get rid of me that easily. Though when it comes to making the beast with two backs, I think
Cracks are beginning to show in my armour. It seems a lot of
Effort's required for someone who's tired before he's even begun,
It's now a major effort to indulge in what used to be fun; pounding heart, aching hips, Plus a fear of an outbreak of wind; and that's just in the run up to doing something I Haven't done in a long, long time.

Luckily, it's not yet a crime to fantasise about a prowess that used to be, the sexual Athlete winning gold in the sex Olympics marathon; now I'd sooner eat one, though I Think they've renamed them 'SNICKERS', which rhymes with...'KICKERS', which Makes me think of bucket,
Oh fuck it.
('SNICKERS' bars used to be called 'MARATHON' for those too young to remember; and those too young to remember, shouldn't be reading adult material, not that it ever stopped me, Heh-heh-heh!!! 24/6/99)

....

INEXORABLE INEVITIBILITY.
20/5/99.

I love the sound of certain words, excluding unguent, emollient, and serendipity; feisty is Another one I don't have much time for either. Neither do I care for pompadour, unlike Troubadour; a word that conjures up a sentiment I adore, of a minstrel strolling along The greenwood track, with his hurdy-gurdy strapped across his back, hoping to arrive At the next castle before dark and the drawbridge hoisted up for the night.

If this were the case as he drew near, he'd call out loud and clear like a Chanticleer, "If It's sweet music you want to hear, then let me in, you need have no fear". And as a taster Of what was to come, he would regale the castle dwellers with the magical and hypnotic Hum from the drone of his wondrous instrument; heralding his intent to entertain them All night long with poetry in song, of courtly love and deeds.

Of derring do; of jousts and knights on quests, such as Sir Gawain; and the blight brought to the Arthurian court by Lancelot and the king's treacherous consort, Quinevere.

All this enthralment in exchange for a few coins and a couple of flagons of beer, and a Chance to sleep near the fire, set in its enormous hearth, with stags, bears, and boars Heads staring out from the walls of the great hall; and a blanket of fur to wrap himself in, holding perhaps, the fleas that brought the 'Black Death'.

....

A FAREWELL TO THE SEAHORSES.
1/2/99.

Water, water everywhere, soon to be as totally contaminated as the
Stagnant air we have no choice but to breathe into our tortured lungs. Already, Polar Bears are being born with hermaphrodite genitalia, because the whole of their food Chain has been poisoned by chemical pollution. There's no quick fix solution can save us Now, the countdown to the end has begun. Luckily for me, I've had the best years of my Life, so I can sit back and watch the destruction of the planet's eco systems with a Perverted sense of fun; I am GOD, passing judgement on the human race; you will see My face in every acid raindrop that slides down your triple-glazed windowpanes. You Will feel my wrath when the last seahorse has been born too deformed to dance in the Oceans; whose motions have been stilled by too many turds from too many people.

(PS. I entered this poem anonymously for 'The Beehive Press poetry comp' '99, they were looking for entries on the theme of water, as well as an entry fee; hence my anonymous feeless entry. I also appended a footnote to my poem which runs: 'You can have this one on me for free as no doubt, with my sentiments you will disagree, and I need my money to buy water purification tablets'.)

(PPS. 25/6/02. On Radio 4's midnight news last night, there was an item about the latest scientific report on the environment, this one from

American doom mongers; they say we're now taking more out of the world's eco systems than can be replaced, we're currently 20% over the Earth's capacity to replace what we're plundering. So now it's a case of waiting and watching for the end of life as we know it; why they can't take lots more water from the oceans is a mystery to me, politicians always moan about the cost, well what price global survival? If we take enough desalinated water out of the oceans, we could re-fertilise the deserts, which we're told are rapidly spreading outwards each passing year; such a plan could also slow down the rising sea levels.

....

THE BRONTE-SAURUS DOTH BORE US.
2/2/99

I hate the Internet, and yet I hate the hype about 'The Brontes" even more.
'WUTHERING HEIGHTS', is a classic case of S&M, and 'JANE EYRE' is just a bore. Branwell

was a junkie, and living in that environment at that phase in human history And development, who could blame him?

I'm sure that if the father of this literary brood were alive today, he'd want to shoo! the Moneygrubbers away from the temple that is Haworth high street; firing curses at their Fleeing feet, and warning them they'll find no place to hide on 'Judgement Day'.

Like everything else, Haworth is dying from the twentieth century blight of too many Sightseers in too many cars, forcing pedestrians into the gutter; it's a pity that the Mutter of discontent from non-polluting walkers doesn't grow into a loud roar of moral Indignation against this creation of the Devil (the car), for lazy bodies and lazy minds; There should be an escalator to ferry us up and down the street instead.

This observation you can have for free; £3 can buy a lot of tins of spaghetti for me, which I eat for my tea. 'DINOSAUR SLAYER'.

(A footnote from the past: I sent this one in anonymously as well, minus the three pounds entrance fee, and now that I've typed it up on my trusty little typewriter, I certainly hope that this is the parting shot for me. I don't want to be a vehicle for the muse any more; if I can't find an outlet for all my finished work then fuck it! I've done, and had enough.

Just think, there are no more manual typewriter's being made anywhere in the world now; I wouldn't swap mine for all the word processors and computers now, over-abundantly in existence, I love it, faults and all...my faults. (Sometime back in 1999.)

PS, Now I'm putting work on disc via my word processor, the best things that I can say about it are, thank fuck for the backspace key, because I'm always pressing the wrong letter keys, and hey! No more finding, or having to pay for ribbons to be changed, it's a technological miracle.

....
....

FOOD FOR THOUGHT, (I'M STARVED FOR CASH.) 4-5/8/99

(Created for the Sue Napolitano Award for disabled writers at Commonword in Manchester. The prize was £10,000, I never expected to win, so I didn't put a serious bid in, 24/8/99 [First mark of the 'loser', not to take matters seriously enough.])

I've never earned £10,000 in one year before, even though I'm two score and ten years And slightly more. I can't imagine going to the food store and not making a mental note f Every penny I spend, shopping with a friend is something I can't afford to do, in case I Lose the plot of what I've got in my basket; and end up red-faced at the till, having to Ask for something to be taken off the bill, so I can pay and make my getaway.

I'm always intrigued by people who manage to fill up their supermarket trolley, if I did That, the contents would last me for a month at least; I'd be having a constant feast of Food to eat before its sell by date, too obese to fasten the top button on my non designer Label jeans. I wish I could live on oven chips and curried beans, digestive biscuits and Tinned rice, very nice for my pocket, but such a repetitive diet might cause me spots and Lots and lots of smelly wind.

Fine words alone don't improve the lives of many people with disabilities, as a disabled Person, all I've ever wanted is normality; it's the able bodied majority who've thwarted Me, constantly putting obstacles in my way, "It's our ball and you can't play, stay on the touchline and admire our skills". "Fuck that", I say.

I haven't got anything positive to say about disability rights issues, I think they only Affect those directly involved. 'New' labour has continued the pogrom of 'welfare to Work'; perhaps I could get a job supervising the, 'Let's put the fear of god into those disabled shirkers' campaign, causing the pain of uncertainty to people like me, who rely On Incapacity benefit for our income.

And now, we've got 'PC' in disability; any note of negativity is more than frowned upon, You and your negative views are socially buried by the 'right on' fascists. Obviously, we Want 'living with dignity' as our natural right, but that won't keep you warm on a cold winter's night; well it won't me anyway. Just because I've got permanently poor Eyesight, doesn't mean I wouldn't be able to hit the mark twice nightly in the dark, if I ever 'copped lucky' again.

You see! Me and my 'mucky' thoughts are detracting from the preciousness that the new social model of disability has elevated itself up to; it regards the able bodied as the disabled now; a bit like the deaf, (not all of them), refusing cochlear implants, and the blind, sorry, 'visually impaired' refusing to see with the help of corrective surgery.

I wish I could earn a minimum of £10,000 every year after tax, and paid, or unpaid sex (at source) was always near, before arthritic 'wear and tear' leaves me too stiff to perform; apart from my willing member that is, who's come to expect a quiet 'fifty off the wrist' as the norm. Oh no! I've just excommunicated myself...again!

(A letter to the adjudicators: I don't expect to qualify in any shape or form for your Sue Napolitano award, it all smacks too much of political correctness to me, and besides, £10,000 isn't that much if you have to come off benefits to earn it, especially if it's taxable.

I'll just add 'FOOD FOR THOUGHT' to my rather large body of unpublished work, and maybe one day I'll be able to self publish, in order to be able to leave something behind me in The British Library; buried within the absolute mass of literature that's already in there.

My name is Philip Louis Fletcher, I'm 52.5 years old, and have only 'partial sight, and increasing problems with arthritic 'wear and tear', as well as periodic depression , [which is more of a threat to my well-being than my physical ailments, though I think they're the contributory factors; is this a classic case of 'the chicken and the egg'?]. I haven't worked for the last 14.75 years, being classified under the old Invalidity benefit rules as 'unrealistically fit for work'; under the revised Incapacity benefit criteria I suppose I'd be categorised as A1 fit, having the use of all my limbs, as well as my brain; although the latter comes under severe strain due to all the hidden pressures I'm subjected to. I should have had a brain haemorrhage (spelling uncertain) (I've just corrected it using 'word search') years ago. I can't understand Tony Blair's zeal in pursuing disabled people, (I know you don't approve of that term, but you're probably able bodied, and it will offend your sensitivities much more than mine); it's not as if the workforce needs us. We've got all these political asylum seekers coming in to the country, looking for work and housing, they can replace the 'smart people' who are leaving the orth in droves to move to sunnier climes and happier times down south.

Thus ends the first and last lesson from me to you, unless you decide you want to give me that ten thousand quid, so I can research the true meaning of the social model of disability in today's complex multicultural Britain, where you can drop yourself in it before you realise you've deeply offended someone, and have to spend the rest of your life watching your back. 23/8/99.

....

A MORBID TRAIN OF THOUGHT.
24/7/99

An immense, deep orange moon rose up from behind the rooftops of the houses at the far end of the street; it would turn bright yellow as it moved higher in its arc across the night sky. The road would be almost blissfully deserted, now the night-time curfew on non essential vehicle usage had come into force; though the hated police helicopter was sure to be prowling about periodically, with its one great white eye and whirring wings; a cross between an angry wasp and an interrogation beam being shone in your eyes.

He'd go for a walk soon with his headphones on, listening to an old jingly jangly riff by U2, the haunting intro to 'I STILL HAVEN'T FOUND WHAT I'M LOOKING FOR'. It always made him feel like dancing in circles, with his arms upraised, paying homage to the magic of the night, and the sense of freedom it invoked; now that those metallic insects had been forced off the roads for a few essential hours. Their drivers were too afraid to walk the streets after dark, afraid of the silence and the calm; they couldn't unwind enough after their frenetic daytime scuttling about, so they stayed in, watching disaster docu-soaps on TV.

He loved this new state of affairs, he was the kerb crawler now; he loathed the new breed of humanity that had forced the authorities to begin taking such drastic actions to try and contain ever increasing levels of air pollution. These hell-bound hedonists who had adopted a blanket philosophy of, "Well, the planet's dying so we might as well get as much selfish pleasure in as we can before it's too late". The type of twats who'd have their two top front teeth pierced if they thought it would keep them ahead in the fashion stakes. He wanted to be the Angel of Death to all of them, painting red crosses on their foreheads to mark them out for retribution, his own fashion statement.

The world, with all its wonderful variety of other life forms, didn't deserve to be sacrificed just so these morons could get their kicks.
If only a virus more virulent than AIDS and drug resistant TB put together, would materialise and begin reducing human numbers at the same rate that they were reducing everything else, before it's too late. This notion that all human life is sacred is a blasphemy. He hoped that anti abortionists would be the first to get wasted, preferably from Ebola; closely followed by the 'politically correct', he'd choose bubonic plague for them, because he liked the sound of it, and he was sure they'd blow their inhuman cover in their delirious death throes.
The moon was high in the distance as he walked the dimly lit pavements, and somewhere out there was Mars, the dead red planet that mad scientists here on Earth thought might contain an amoeba or two, still lurking in the long extinct canal beds; and were prepared to spend precious billions of dollars to prove it. Life-blood money that was being drained from the only living jewel in the known universe, 'Let whatever they find prove toxic to them', he fervently prayed.
Scientists were to blame for this horrendous explosion in human numbers, they were eradicating too many diseases too fast; even atomic bombs being dropped couldn't stem this lethal tide. Why was the global population increasing so relentlessly? Why are these amorphous masses breeding out of control?

They're not the enlightened people of the western world, that's for sure.
Ultimately, Nature will be the great leveller he thought smugly, as he took a swig from his comfort bottle of wine, and inhaled toxic smoke into his complaining lungs; he had his own death wish to satisfy.
Human locusts being reduced to feeding on plagues of locusts and lemmings, rats and scorpions, as well as fat juicy pregnant tarantula spiders, and pulsating grubs pulled out of the ground; and finally and most fitting of all, each other! It was almost dawn before his head hit the pillow, he slept immediately.

26/8/99. My nose has been bleeding loads of watery snot while I've been typing this up, I've contacted a really stinking head cold after going to Halifax yesterday to look at the council flat on offer. The weather was wet and misty, I've decided not to take the flat (on the 17th floor), but stick it out here till I can afford to move to another private house; more snot's just dripped onto my precious typewriter.

26/6/02. Update on the above. Due to being 'screwed' by everyone I come into contact with, apart from Gail, I've ended up in a spatially-challenged council bungalow in outer Todmorden; which is just as well really, because I hate housework and I've no more worries about being overcharged by plumbers and various other members of the building trade. The scenery's quite nice also, and I have a small back garden, which the council come and cut the grass of for me.

PPS. I was eventually hounded out of this hovel by teenage hobgoblins off the estate; they did me a massive favour really, if only I hadn't been moved into a flat with a fucking dance school on top of it, here in sunny, unfunny Halifax. 1/7/06.

....

OH TO BE INTERESTING.
3/8/99

Oh to be interesting and in demand, to have some 'top totty' drooling at my feet, and paparazzi lurking in the bushes outside my house, waiting for a shot of my V-fingered salute, or the outspread feet of my latest conquest protruding from the backseat window of my newest car; with my mooning buttocks jammed in-between, wobbling their way to the promised land of perpetual orgasm, which only lasts a short, jerking spasm here on Earth.
Oh for a rebirth from the social decline into which I've sunk, I couldn't be less popular if I was a stench emitting skunk, and I'm just as amorous as 'Pierre Le Phew'; too romantically inclined for my

own good, that's why I'm always pulling my pud; Mrs Palmer and her five lovely daughters never complain if a shower of warm spunky rain gets smeared all over them. It's been so long since my knob's been where it's meant to be, in that hotbed of intrigue and mystery, that it's got segs on it from too much self abuse; it's grown knobbly. Things will probably remain this way, unless I can make a breakthrough in this overcrowded land of 'wannabes', some of them only come up to my knees, but they're really pushy. Warbling away with the voices of angels while mine's more like 'Lurch' out of 'THE ADAMS FAMILY', maybe I've been permanently knocked off my perch in this overly age-conscious society of ours?

....
.....

SOULLESS SEX. (IT MUST BE GREAT FOR PEOPLE WITH NO SOULS.) 25/7/99

You might as well be amoebas copulating (if they do), soulless sex is so cold-blooded and calculating. It's acceptable for the callous, uncaring young, for they're allowed to make mistakes as long as they don't mind coping with the rigours of herpes, thrush, unwanted pregnancies and the trauma of abortion, or even the dreaded HIV.

Me? I'm looking down the tunnel of lovelessness that's been my life, an ever widening vortex, sadly, slowly spinning to infinity, made up from all the days, colours, textures, and emotions of my life.

It's mostly dusky grey in colour, with flashes of streetlight orange, summer sky blue, deep orange pavements and black tree leaf shadows, electric reds, blues, greens, yellows, pale violets; images of timeless landscapes and ancient houses, dry stone walls and cobbled roads, emotions as scarred as any rock face.

I want to be able to float back down this tunnel of loveless time and glean what I can from its walls of my memories. There was a sense of newness and wonder there that I can no longer feel or find, only a longing for that lost magic, that sense of youthful freedom.

The wild, vibrant flare-up of autumn colours giving way to the barren browns and greys of winter, hard to see stars through our nebulous and unforgiving night skies, the warm expectation of house lights as you approach in a storm, followed by unutterable desolation as you pass by, cold and soaked to the skin. The desire to be a part of Nature while at the same time detesting being over exposed to the elements.

The struggle to resist total disinterest in everything, while simultaneously remaining breathing; and the need to resist hating too much.

A sense of bafflement at how all other animals

function without the advantage of a vocabulary and thought process as we understand it, and do it successfully too.

I want to live too long, because I'm afraid that death has nothing to offer. That paradise is merely a carrot on the end of a stick to entice us into an abyss of total blackness and silence. Better to exist in a lonely, slow-moving vortex, with traces of indigo and deep violet in its dusky grey coils to match my moods of injustice and pain; as searching and introspective as Shostokovic's Tenth Symphony, and as lovely and haunting as Holst's 'VENUS' from 'THE PLANETS SUITE'; and just as elusive and unattainable.

Having nothing relevant to say anymore with so many ways of saying it, while ill health eats my life away, my silent screams bouncing off the walls of my vortex; filling great and darkened halls with emptiness. The cold winds of imminent death blowing through the cracks in the walls. Perhaps the only way to avoid death is to become totally enmeshed in my vortex, encircling it like ectoplasm, trapping dull death inside, like an evil fly in the web of a defiant giant red spider, with hissing rows of hollow teeth.

The angry Phil Fletcher.

....

BUBOES.

I've given myself permission to go insane, time and time again.
To do what I will and feel no guilt, to wreak revenge on the tormentors who have turned my inner sanctuary into a place of torture and pain.

....

SMOKE GETS UP YOUR NOSE.   13/8/99.

If you stick a 'tab' or cigar in the corner of your mouth, like Clint Eastwood did in the Spaghetti Westerns trilogy, smoke gets up your nose. I tried sticking a tab in the corner of my gob a few times in the bad old days when I smoked regularly; I always found the smoke going up my nose really irritating, and never lasted a full tab; I think prolonged fag dangling activity could cause lip cancer, imagine having your lips removed!!??

....

NICE-LOOKING AND VOLUPTUOUS GOLD-DIGGERS WELCOME.   21/6/99.

I used to be in love with love, but now I'm in love with money, it could open every door to the wish fulfilment I'm longing for. It might not be able to buy me love but it could provide me with the next best thing; three in a bed sex romps in Bangkok or Rome. If I had sufficient cash I could buy the home I'd love to own, a stylish house with a drive, and the grounds and lawns are kept tidy by a man a lot like myself, trustworthy but at the same time ambitious and money-hungry; he'd have to mow a really neat lawn or I'd sack the bastard without pay on his final trial day.
It looks like I'm paving the way to my personal hell, selling my soul for mammon; well it's been malnourished for a long time now anyway. And if, unlike Faust, I'm unable to cheat the Devil on soul redemption day, I'll be in good company down below, Judas Iscariot and Marilyn Monroe.
I'm glad I wasn't one of the hapless 46, who each, for a little while, thought they'd won the jackpot after matching up the six numbers required in last week's national lottery draw; I bet it was more than their faces that hit the floor when they found out they were going to only get a 46th share of the 7.1 million pound pot; the lucky thirteen who matched 5 numbers plus the bonus ball were in line to win more than them, a phenomenon never to happen again, (not so far anyway.)

It's enough to make me like even REM, who I hope will go to heaven and not to hell, I'd hate to bump into Mr 'slaphead' Micheal Stypes and his 'right-on' crew down there, unless I had a red hot poker in my hand to give a roastingly hot welcome to the band.

Speaking of sand, which I know I wasn't, the number of sperms that have come in my hand over the years, must be equal in amount to the number of grains surrounding Blackpool pier. They'd have been of much more value to me if deposited in a sperm bank; but honestly speaking, I don't think my semen's worth a wank; if each minute DNA chip is as traumatised as me then I'm happy to draw a blank over the whole procreative farce; I'll happily spend the rest of my natural on my arse, 'Feeling it coming in the air tonight'.

Money could put a healthier slant on this morbid train of thought, if I had plenty of it I could call up an escort at times when I was feeling horny, the interest on my large account would pay for her time, so in a way I'd be getting it for FREE! That makes sound financial sense to me, and appeals to my sense of morals too; women who otherwise wouldn't give me the time of day going away thinking I was paying them out of my own 'pocket rocket' fund, when in reality it wasn't me paying them at all, I was getting my 'jollies' for FUCKALL!

And, if after all my cash assisted excesses, my health began to fail, I'd be straight into private health care, not some NHS gaol with its average two year waiting list to get in, against a much more frequent breakout of Ecoli 157 and other food poisoning, literally! Have you tasted NHS hospital food? It's as crude as the hygiene standards the overworked and underpaid cleaners try to maintain, who, ironically, get paid the same as the sorely oppressed junior doctors who are often so tired, they leave your wounds poorly dressed.

If money is indeed the square root of all evil, then the struggle for its supremacy is already won, 'Greed is good' is the whole of the law, and you are at liberty to seek your fill of it. "Eyes down, look in, it's everyone for themselves, and the Devil take the hindmost, which he usually does. Crack heads, smack heads, and hookers with the clap and much worse, which reminds me of a joke: 'She was only the poet's daughter, but she said she wasn't averse".

(Author's note. I read this modern poem out at a public reading held at The Hourglass Studio in Hebden Bridge, during that town's art festival this summer (1999), just before the interval, most of the audience never came back; I regard this as a compliment.)

....

ON THE EDGE. (HOW CAN I LOVE YOU IF YOU'RE NOT HERE?)   5/8/99.

I live on the edge of society, unwanted because of poverty and disability, a bit like an STD: sexually transmitted disease; only I find it much more difficult to communicate with the opposite sex than this clinging strain of social perfidy.
I've had this hex on me since birth, not being taken for what I'm worth, as well as personality; (?), but being marked down as a potential bad risk for a bride to give birth to my offspring; which I don't want to inflict on the world either, there are enough facially challenged people already around to spoil your view of the human zoo.
Yet this doesn't stop me suffering the pangs of unrequited desire, my libido's on fire every time I go out; I feel like a beast in search of prey, a sexual indiscretion is only a moment of madness away. A custodial sentence is something I shouldn't have to pay for wanting to do what comes naturally, but which has been denied me; I'm in purgatory. I can see and smell the sweets but I can't have any.
Now, like a lot of rejected adult males, I have a jaundiced view, how do I love 'You' when you're

not there? Like a plate of iron filings mixed with bits of barbed wire, eaten with exposed nerve endings in my teeth? Or my own house on fire and 'you' inside it on a funeral pyre? Or a dish of carnivorous worms who've just devoured their mild mannered counterparts, the humble but very useful earthworm? What would make me squirm even more, would be a bucket of hissing puff adders, served up for me to choose one to be skinned alive before my starting eyes, in a restaurant run by Thais.

I could love 'you' if your open thighs were at my disposal whenever I felt the need to feed my sex starved life. I could love 'you' even more if you were my wife, twenty years younger than myself; please take me off this dust, and cobweb-filled shelf, whoever 'you' are, I'll name a star after 'you' like Curly Watts did for Raquel, if 'you'll' end my lonely hell and say, "Yes, you can come and play the dating and mating game with me". Ecstasy that I can only fantasise about right now, beneath 'Love's Labours Lost', leafless bough.

> (A. N. (geddit?) I actually sent this dubious effort in for a yucky love poetry comp', along with a cheque for three quid! What a MUG! No wonder I never heard anything back from the conning gets, serves me right for feeling vulnerable and exposed, emotionally. 27/6/02.)

....
.....

PHYSICAL CORRECTNESS. (PUTTING THE 'EVIL EYE' IN ITS PROPER PERSPECTIVE.) 30/10/99.

Safeguarding my privacy and my property is of the utmost importance to me; I spend a lot of time alone in my home. But I'm never really on my own thanks to the weird and warped attentions of some of the inbred 'local', yokels who've developed the 'sixth sense' to a fine art. They know how to tear my privacy apart by striking at the very heart of it, such as the twat next door slamming a door right when there's a lull in some music I'm really enjoying; destroying my ecstatic mood completely. Or, some lame-brained retard spurring its phallic symbol into loud action by masturbating its engine outside my house.
These kind of interruptions turn this normally placid mouse into an impotently roaring lion; this scion of the king of beasts has to content himself with bursts of vitriolic invective against these 'perps', shouted through the wall or through the window, in-between dyspeptic burps brought on by my discomposed equilibrium,

Such is the hostile atmosphere (for me) round here, that I live in fear of a brick coming through my living room window every time I stand near it, and the frequent appearance of dog shit on my doorstep or the pavement outside my place, puts a grimace on my face when I have to clean it up; as well as the chip supper papers, trays and cans; is this an orchestrated plan to wear me down, or merely a random campaign of urban terror?
But these petty acts of harassment are as nothing compared to the malevolent ESP that 'watches' me even when I'm away from here. The 'long viewing' that lets me know by burning sensations in either ear, whether it approves or resents what I'm doing. It's cold fire for hate and an arid blast of hot desert wind for what passes from it as love; my ears are highly sensitive to these violations of my human rights to privacy, especially in the inner sanctuary of my mind.
I've tried to unravel and unwind the motives behind this palpable evil, but so far I've drawn a blank. Is there a satanic coven that wants to bend me to its will? I'd die before I'd let that happen, they've got nothing that I want, they see everything inside out and back to front; I'm not so desperate for a bit of cunt that I'd consort with such verminous trash; soulless sex is merely a flash in their deadpan world of servitude and bondage. Judging by the sulphurous reek, which all too often accompanies the gas that escapes from my painfully bloated insides, I'd say that something evil therein abides, a demonic tapeworm perhaps,

or an insatiable succubus that would rather feed off my waste matter than 'sleep' with me in my sleep, (nothing unusual there then). I wish I could lure it out so I could batter it to death, a squealing, squelching red thing, writhing on the carpet till I could kill it; and then have it taken away to be dissected by Peter Cushing and Christopher Lee. I hope it wouldn't eat its way out through my vest like that hideous little alien in the film of the same name, I couldn't stand the shame of being found with a dirty thermal one on with sweat stains beneath my armpits, and a terminal case of the 'squits' nestling in, and disgracing my underpants, clean on that morning...honest.

....

SUICIDE ISN'T PAINLESS, UNLIKE THE SONG, WHICH WAS PAINFUL TO LISTEN TO. 11/10/99.

You have to be hurting pretty bad inside to even think about it.
The thought of hanging, or going under a train, makes my brain squirm in anguish. Better to languish in the knowledge that you're going to die one day anyway, so why rob yourself of all that additional heartache and pain? If you're lucky

you'll demise prematurely from all the emotional strain you've put yourself through.

A truly heaven and hellish way to disintegrate is through a love/hate relationship with drink and pills; the drink to enhance your glorious wallowing in self pity, and the pills to cure your ills from the drinking; this can work okay till you wake up one day thinking you've died and gone straight to HELL!! Well, maybe it's best to cut your throat if it gets like that, or microwave the cat and eat it with all its fur on, that'll give you something to choke on.

Choking apart, it's agonising to hear of young people needlessly dying because they find life too trying, it doesn't matter so much if old farts like me have had enough; but my advice to anyone under thirty suffering too much turmoil would be, 'Hold on, learn to take the smooth with the rough, death is forever, you'll be dead soon enough'.

....

THERE'S NO MUSIC TO MURDER.   27-8/10/99

I'm having an 'at home' alone this evening, so I can give my sparkling, infectious, and lovable personality the night off. I'm so deliciously charming it's alarming; I attract people like flies.

If I was as promiscuous as everyone thinks I am, I'd have friction burns on my inner thighs.
I don't know why I feel the need to effervesce the way I do, but put me in a social setting and it's my cue to go, 'Yoo-hoo! I'm over here'! I'm giving off signals of potential availability fit to burst, it's my thirst for wanting to be popular and desirable that I constantly need to satisfy. Yet inside, I have a morbid fear of being on my own with anyone; if I throw a party I'm always glad when they've all gone. I don't allow sycophants to cling on to me; everyone thinks everyone else is having me, I hope they don't all find out at once that none of them are. It could cause the more determined ones to lay siege to my door, promising true love and fidelity forever more if I'll only let them in. There's no fear of that, well not till the wrinkles and grey hair have really begun to appear, I'm happy in my penthouse flat and management consultancy position, it's the best thing since medium sliced bread. 'Do as we say or your company's dead in the water, and our fees will slaughter your profit margin'.
Tonight I'm watching television with my feet up, 'THERE'S NO MUSIC TO MURDER' is on again for the umpteenth time; but I don't mind, it's my favourite film noir, highlighting my favourite film star, Humphrey Eastwood as a cigar-smoking private dick. His performance is slick, yet with a raw and dangerous edge, especially when he dangles his unfaithful girlfriend from a window ledge 30 storeys high, and forces her to confess her

reasons why, before he allows her to fly briefly into space, with that sardonic smirk on his face that he's so well remembered for.

"Here's looking at you creep", he'd lazily say before blowing some perp away with the most powerful hand gun in the world, knowing he could get away with it because he had a licence to kill in the all American way of, 'WANTED, DEAD OR ALIVE', preferably dead. It saved time and lawyers fees that way, and the reward money would help boost his irregular pay of fifty dollars a day plus expenses.

I know it's terribly un-PC of me, but someone like him could cut right through my defences and roger me till he made my eyes water, to the devil a willing daughter I'd be; it's just as well no-one can see what I'm doing now in front of the TV, except me in the overhead mirror above my couch, OUCH! I'd forgotten I'd left that earring there.

....
....

WLTM. (WOULD LIKE TO MEET, A GROTESQUE HORROR STORY.) 1-4/9/99

The dead try to reach out to each other through their senses from the cold, clammy, smelly confines of their coffins in the lonely and deserted graveyard. Well, at least I do, I've been dead for some time now; I've had no luck so far but I'll keep on trying, I've got nothing else to do with my endless time.
At first I couldn't believe it, I thought my suicide attempt had failed and I was swathed in cold wet bandages from head to foot, and I'd burnt my eyes out and my nose, lips and ears off; it was so silent and so black, as black as jet and as heavy as the ocean five miles down. And just as terrifying at first, till I realised I wasn't breathing nor needed to. I seem to be a state of mind inside a rotting corpse in a coffin, with a couple of tons of soggy earth on top of me; why couldn't they have cremated me and finished the job off properly that I'd started?
When I first understood I wasn't in a severe state of self inflicted illness in a hospital somewhere, but actually dead, I went insane for a time, I've always been claustrophobic, I thrashed around in my coffin as much as a gaseous substance can do; anyway, no-one could have heard my screams even if I would have had a voice to emit them with.
i can only assume that the small amount of air trapped inside my coffin when the lid was being

screwed down, plus the gases being released by my charred, decomposing corpse, are what's keeping me 'alive'. I certainly don't need air to breathe, I am merely a thought process; in a macabre way the gasses being passed by my rotting remains are being purified by being filtered through my charcoal shell; all in all it's not as unpleasant in here as at first I assumed it was going to be, apart from the rumblings and gurglings going on as the fluids and substances break down. But I had plenty of embarrassing noises to put up with while I was alive, so I don't get too depressed about my overall situation...anymore.

I'm even able to sleep after a fashion; I go into a state of suspended animation, a kind of self-hypnosis. I always needed a lot of sleep while I was alive, it was my way of coping with tedium, and I had plenty of that to put up with; I had a low tedium threshold. I seemed to get depressed or dispirited very easily, and escaping off to bed was my way of coping. Once I realised I didn't have big league potential I more or less gave up, there was none of the 'Eddie the Eagle' tenacity about me, 'If at first you don't succeed, give up', was my unspoken motto, or 'If it doesn't come easy, it's not worth having'.

I had a nasty habit of thinking of all the things that could go wrong in any venture I was interested in, and would end up doing nothing. I used to resist this unpleasant trait when I was younger, and would go ahead with the resulting disappointing fiasco; but over the ensuing years I became less and less inclined to put my fragile ego at risk, and eventually gave up trying altogether. My existence became a siege against harsh reality, even going to the shops was a burdensome ordeal; the only things I enjoyed were music, watching TV, and reading. But in the end, even my love for these entertaining pastimes waned, and I came to the disillusioned and embittered conclusion that my life was more trouble than it was worth.

Once I'd come to this dramatic and devastating realisation, matters seemed a lot simpler, if I wanted to end this unenviable state of affairs I could do. No more feelings of guilt born out of a sense of failure and inadequacy, no more shaving to keep the white hairs at bay, no more half-hearted attempts at housework; who'd have thought that endeavouring to keep on top of a bit of dirt and grime, albeit very spasmodically, could be so physically and mentally exhausting?

No more loneliness, and most significantly of all, no more me! It felt uncanny how easily a plan for my own self-destruction came to me, I've heard of indecent haste but this was almost insultingly quick. The idea of killing myself came to me late on a Friday night, the start to one more horrendously boring weekend; so by the Monday morning I'd worked it all out. I didn't just want to kill myself, I wanted to obliterate everything I'd held dear, even the money I'd painstakingly saved; I was going to turn my home into a funeral pyre, using all my writings, books, and savings as fuel.

It occurred to me that attempting to burn my house down with me in it, I could settle a couple of scores. The neighbours on either side of me had never been very neighbourly to me since I'd moved in; in fact they'd been downright hostile, probably adding momentum to this, my ultimate decision. If the blaze became intense enough it might make their houses unsafe and they'd have to move out, that should upset and infuriate the fuckers. At the very least they'd be sorely discomfited for a few hours while the fire brigade damped down my smouldering ruin.

So I set about withdrawing my modest savings over a period of days, and buying four litres of 5-Star Napoleon Brandy, no cheap and nasty petrol for me. I intended to go out in style. My plan was hopefully, to choke to death on smoke fumes from the conflagration, a few hundred feet of cassette tape should provide some nice toxic fumes. I was going to be well primed with brandy by the time the fire was fully alight, the combination of that and poisonous gases should see me off before any flames could get to me, and burn me alive.

The mood of cold determination stayed with me as the days unfolded, no sentimental back-pedalling was allowed to creep in; at last I'd found my 'raison d'etre', and nothing short of a miracle was going to undermine my resolve. A welcoming smile from an attractive, unattached female might have persuaded me to change my mind, especially if accompanied by the hint of a possible relationship, like I'd read so often in the over-demanding columns in the singles ads; 'WLTM tall, dark, handsome male, preferably over 6ft tall, solvent and house trained. Own house, car, hair and teeth a massive bonus. Must really enjoy eating out, foreign travel, and picking up the tab for both of us. Possible shag when I'm pissed for the right mug. Me? I've been round the track a few times, and look okay in a dim light after you've had a skinful. I smoke, have no cash that you'll ever see, enjoy shopping with my friend while my man's out earning the cash to keep me sweet, so if you're dumb enough to fit these requirements, and desperate enough to respond, you're the sucker for me'.

One of my unrequited ambitions had been to be a male escort, getting lonely unattached women to pay me to accompany them on nights out, and later, pay me again to have sex with them to round the evening off nicely. I think the only relevant requirements I possessed were 'own hair and teeth', and I'm quite tall, all my other assets were either dropping off or rusting up, and my eyesight had always been crap; another big nail in my coffin. So the longed for smile never came, unlike 'D' day, death day that is. I planned not to set the fire till 1:am to make sure it would remain undetected for as long as possible, so I just had a normal day, eating when I was hungry, watching the telly, counting all my paper cash.

I relished the prospect of a pauper's grave, a bit like the disgraced 'Mayor of Casterbridge'; I had relatives who I hoped would not be traceable by the authorities. I began drinking my brandy at 11 pm, I wanted to be well 'ratted' by the time I lit my funeral pyre, with just enough of my wits left about me to make it to the top of my cosy little open plan house. In my downstairs living room I had a very roomy armchair, I'd torn up all my writings, even my diaries, (not without a few twinges of nostalgic regret), and ripped my money up with a sense of satisfaction that no-one else would benefit from my self denial in saving it, and draped the difficult to remove cassette tape, (it occurred to me after my struggle that video tape was much easier to extract, how typical of me), round the chair after I'd made a big pile of my life's work in the seat. I tacked a blanket over the double glazed window to prevent as much of the flame light as possible from being seen too soon; I was going to leave the lights on, but just in case. I deactivated the smoke alarms, and tore up all my favourite authors in paperback, (I just don't see the point of publishing hardback books anymore, I'd never buy one, the price of them; and the extra material needed to produce them is so harmful to the environment) to make a trail up the two flights of stairs to my bedroom/study; there was no bedroom door to keep the smoke out for too long, that's what I meant by 'open plan'. I was going to use three litres of brandy to douse the place enough to get the fire well started, I wanted it to go up like a huge Christmas pudding, with me listening to 'THE END' by 'THE (fabulous) DOORS' when my end came; and that's what more or less happened. I diluted my brandy with ersatz ginger ale, I didn't want to get drunk too soon, or feel nauseous. I was going to play my DOORS CDs and smoke rollups like I did when I was young; I'd had a love/hate relationship with smoking for the past twelve years of my life, that last night I loved it.

As I got into the music, especially 'WHEN THE MUSIC'S OVER', which it shortly would be for me, I began a brief resume' of my life, a painful process. It was all aborted relationships and dead end brick walls; I did believe that a malevolent deity ruled my fate, and this was my last chance to stick two fingers up to the evil bastard! I love 'THE DOORS', and all my old favourites sounded better than ever that last time of listening. About 12.30 am, I had a preliminary listen to 'THE END', and when Jim Morrison was intoning the apocalyptic words: 'The killer awoke before dawn, he put his boots on and he walked on down the hall', I thought of all the people who'd dumped on me, and who I often fantasised about meting out retribution to. When he came to the crescendo of the dirge and was chanting: 'Kill, Kill, Kill!', my left hand was making involuntary stabbing motions; time to light my fire in time to 'THE DOORS': 'LIGHT MY FIRE'.

I pulled the chair near to the first flight of stairs and groggily dropped a burning rag on it with the words "Burn, mother burn" on my lips, and it did; the brandy-soaked paper went up with a WHOOSH! I almost singed my hair, and I hate that particular smell. Once the chair took hold the fire would soon spread; I really gulped the brandy down then and positioned myself at the top of the second flight of stairs to wait for the smoke to come up. I reckon it took less than five minutes for the heat and smoke to begin rising up to me, and the merry sound of the flames was reassuring. The smoke, grey at first, soon turned black, it came bubbling up the stairs like the dark ghost I used to terrify myself with when I was a kid, it smelt like burning rubber.

I heard the words: 'Lost in a roman wilderness of pain' as I took my first lungful, and threw up straightaway; my head was spinning out of control as I automatically gulped for air, in-between retching. I began to choke. That was the most unpleasant part that I can remember, clutching at my throat with only the black acrid smoke to inhale. I went reeling round the room with Jim Morrison shouting, 'Kill, Kill, Kill!' again, and my own strangled voice gurgling, "Come on death damn you, do your worst, let's get this lugubrious affair that's been my existence over with". (I'd always wanted to use the word 'lugubrious' to good effect and this had been my chance.) The last words I heard were: 'The end of nights we tried to die', just above the roar of the flames; I think I heard loud banging on my front door as well, but that was it, I disappeared down that final black hole, from where I've rematerialised in this unwholesome state, death had done its worst by leaving me in this undead reincarnation, trapped six feet below ground.

Well, I've developed a routine now, almost a routine for survival. I cast around with my mind to see if I can detect any other poor unfortunates, hoping to make contact. Then I try and concentrate on some nice memory, a country lane in the early morning sunlight for instance, or the trace of orgasm running through Wagner's Liebestod Overture, or I 'sleep' as much as possible. Perhaps one day this cemetery will be dug up and our rotted coffins dumped on to the grass. If the lid of mine comes off, there'll be a rush of fetid air, accompanied by the echo of a scream, and I'll be free to infiltrate myself into the unsuspecting body of a living host, through its mouth!!!

(A tour de force if ever I wrote one, I wonder if I'd need permission from 'THE DOORS', minus Jim of course, to reproduce all reference to their music? It would be a privilege to have Ray Manzerek read this piece of esoteric existentialism.)

(3/7/06. I misguidedly entered this story into a short story competition for Calderdale Library earlier this year. Imagine my indignation when I didn't even get in the first 3 winners of their poxy comp'. I sent a blistering note of complaint in and managed to get my copy of this piece returned to me; like I said, the judge must have had no taste.

Quite possibly I'll be saying the same thing later this year, after I've failed yet again in my attempt to win the £5000 1st prize in the Bridport Arts Poetry Comp', with my intriguingly titled entry: 'POETRY IS DEAD!', and with a judge named Lavinia Greenlaw, I'll be very surprised if my diatribe isn't dead in the water moments after she's read it. (It cost me 6 quid to enter as well, a calculated risk.)

....

THE GRAVE ROBBER.
7-16/11/99

My mind can't conceive of a state of not being, which is what death might well be. It recoils from the brink of the abyss and huddles for warmth and shelter deep inside me.
I want to rob the grave of my presence for as long as possible, just like those shrivelled old ladies who barely seem to have enough strength to drag themselves round on their sticks to the shops, but have a tenacious look in their eye that says, 'I'll outlive you matey'; and you know, I think they'll try. It's them who are a drain on the public purse, stubbornly staying above ground when they should have been in a hearse long ago; still having

the gall to collect their pensions, which they hide in cupboards and in drawers, it's no wonder they're afraid to open their doors for fear of being pushed over by the slightest mugger, posing as their long lost son. And when they can't put it off any longer, they take longer to burn in the crematorium furnace because there's not enough fat left on them to help reduce them to ash quicker.

Someone said (it was 'Father Ted' actually), that the needy 'are a shower of bastards', I should know, I'm one of them. I need state benefits to keep me alive, I need lots of love and affection, which the state can't provide. I have to hide my needs in longing for something, or someone nice to turn up...before my toes do. Some people aren't meant to find the fame and fortune they think they so richly deserve in their own lifetime; they get 'discovered' when they're mouldering in the grave, and will have to wait till Judgement Day before they can be judged worthy of their posthumous reputations.

There's a well known blues song with a line that goes: 'If it wasn't for bad luck I wouldn't have no luck at all', I'd like to adapt that to, 'If it wasn't for junk mail, I wouldn't get no mail at all', or, 'If it wasn't for meter readers and double glazing 'cold callers', I wouldn't get any callers at all'.

....
....

A CHRISTMAS CAROL RE-EVALUATED.
14-16/11/99

Tiny Tim's well and truly dead, and Scrooge is off his head from being under attack from too much pre-Christmas advertising; Bob Cratchit can't reach round to scratch it, and the ghost of Christmas Present isn't bothering this year. Lucky revellers are singing, 'Oh, we're going to Barbados, and we don't envy the poor turkeys who're stopping here'. Fears of global warming and world famine won't put a blight on my festive mood, I'll be stuffing my face with food that I think is going to poison me, unless it's cooked till it's almost on fire; and I'll be higher than a kite on Christmas cheer, wine, brandy, and beer. Santa help me on boxing day if I'm still able to breathe, my stomach will be seething with bile, and my head will be like a sieve till millennium eve, when the whole process will have to be gone through again; actually, I don't think I could stand the pain of this double celebration. I'd rather be alert so I could hit the January sales, which now start on Dec. 26th, and buy myself all the 'crimbo pressies' I so well deserve, at knockdown prices.
I won't even think of the emotional crisis I'm permanently having from being lonely and lovelorn; I've sworn off modern English women anyway, they're far too self-centred, or else they're

away with the fairies on some boring altruistic cause, opposing the breeding of cats with claws, and genetically modified starch. Where have all the lewd and lascivious ones gone? Gone to 'HEDONISM' in Jamaica every one, to have some rude fun in the sun.

The ghost of Christmas yet to come. Phil Fletcher.

LOVE MAGIC, HOW TO MAKE IT DISAPPEAR. 4/7/99

Love magic, when you can't find it, it's tragic. Soulless sex is a poor substitute, but even that's eluded me for a long time now. I have a ravenous, unrequited lust for lovely-looking women, albeit that those looks are merely a lure to attract a mate to procreate. Well that's okay, I don't have any qualms with that, I was born to do it all the time, I should have gone through a whole harem by now; but 'god' committed the ultimate crime against me, causing me to be born 'an ugly thing in a pretty world'.

I have a face more suited to the Apache nation than the refined European strain, I have something of the mien of long dead Apache warrior Chiefs: Mangus Colorado and Cochise; a spiritual affinity and a cruel streak when roused, tempered with an ability to reason that the best

way to deal with the human condition is to distance yourself from it as much as possible.
Who knows how long the Apache nations had been in existence before the hated whites came, and reduced them to the status of scavengers in their own country, forcing their leaders to make a last desperate stand? In defeat and disillusionment becoming impoverished and unhealthily fat, from a flat and destructive diet, too demoralised even to ghost dance.

I long to ride in the deserts and mountain fastnesses that were their home, and live like they did before the alien invaders came and broke them down. I'd like to go and breathe some fire back into the Apache heart, and encourage them to live apart from mainstream America, which is tearing itself apart from within. A mongrelised hotchpotch of the world's hungry and poor, the amorphous masses washed up on the shore of the once proud 'red' Indian homeland.

Even the whites now, who caused America's first inhabitants total defeat, are in retreat from ever increasing numbers of other races. If you don't have national cohesion in a federal system such as hers, sooner or later you can expect the worst, a loss of identity and 'the American way'. Maybe one day the 'pilgrim fathers' will feel as sorely oppressed as the Apaches once did, and their grievances will be hid behind white sheets and burning crosses, lamenting the loss of their proud independence to sheer weight of numbers.

And then the ghosts of the murdered Native American dead will return and dance ecstatically beneath immense iridescent skies, beating drums and singing high, 'Die, all you unbidden intruders, die'! And the stampeding hooves of all the slaughtered buffalo will reverberate through the cities, now filled with fear and hate, and the empire state building will come crashing down, destroying the statue of liberty in a knock on effect; it's only a mocking symbol parodying the cause for freedom anyway. If the red man hadn't betrayed his fellow red man to help the white blight, the need for that accursed statue need never have arisen, and 'America', already populated, remained relatively undisturbed, (like Canada is today for some strange reason.)

If I could choose any time and place in history to have been born, it would have been as a full-blooded Chiricahua Apache warrior long before the white man or the Spaniard came; I'd have had no knowledge of the horror that was to be visited on my native land. Maybe I'd have waged war on neighbouring tribes like we'd always done, staking the more unfortunate ones out beneath the baking sun with their eyelids peeled off. And if I'd lived long enough to die a natural death, I wouldn't have been buried in the ground, or my body sent up in smoke, my human remains would have been embalmed and wrapped in ceremonial buffalo robes and placed on a dais several feet above the earth, so that even in death I would have been in harmony with Nature, gradually disintegrating into timeless time. But my spirit would be roaming free, perhaps waiting for me to be born into this god-forsaken age, to act as a sage for my forgotten people.   (Completed 8/7/99.)

....

Thursday, 9/9/99, 3.45pm by my watch, the three quarter hour is marked by a nine as well, amazing huh?
Well it's another of those EUREKA! Thank fuck I've finished moments, which I really want to be true now. I don't want to write any more. (Readers of the yet to be published DOWN IN ONE will eventually know this wasn't the case; oh, and I've got DEEPER THAN NOTHINGNESS to put out as well), if only to avoid the backbreaking strain of sitting in front of my remarkable and trusty typewriter for hours at a time, typing the stuff out. How the pulp writers do it I'll never know, unless they use cocaine, and like I unpopularly maintain, there's far too much 'product' in existence already; and most of it hardly gets looked at because people haven't the time to devote to it, or keep up with it.
If I live long enough, I'll see my work in book form, even if I have to (and it's looking more and more likely), pay for that privilege myself; I might even develop some confidence to do performance

reading, especially WLTM (WOULD LIKE TO MEET), a bit like Dickens reading the murder scene from Oliver Twist.   1st July 2002ad.

93/7/06. And now I'm opting to put my work on the Internet, for sale as 'e-books' instead of all that paper stuff; and I want to remain as anonymous as possible to, there are far too many thin-skinned people with sharpened axes to grind, only too willing to chop you to bits these days. Just last weekend I read an article in The Daily Mail about a writer who managed to upset vegetarians of all people; a disgruntled group of them caused him a lot of inconvenience, the fucking barmy carrot-munching weirdo's; can you imagine if it had been Vegans he'd upset? I used to know one who was really waspish and vindictive, and as tight as a fish's arsehole, and as mad as a box of frogs; and a cheating, lying con artist…THE BITCH!)

………………………………………………………
……….

BOOK COVER LAYOUT

FRONT COVER, TITLE
COPING WITH MADNESS. (STATEMENTS IN RHYME, SOME OF THE TIME.)

See back cover for glowing 'golden balls' type 'teste'monials.

PHIL FLETCHER (NUT GONE AND FLAKING.)

This publication is not for those of an over sensitive or 'PC' disposition.

Book dedication, inside cover.
To Lucy and Emma who I met on a train, totally alive and totally insane, they never even knew my name; sadly I'll never see either of them again.

BACK COVER, CREDITS.

Phil Fletcher is the Clint Eastwood of the written word, tough and uncompromising.
AXMUS SMOE.

I haven't been so impressed with a new publication since 'VIEWED WITH SUSPICION' came out last year.   **NORGUS NRIMBY.**

Mr Fletcher is a storyteller and plotter after my own heart, which he's threatened to rip out, along with my liver, if I don't say something nice about his 'book'.   **GASTROID THROTTER.**

This man's an undiscovered literary genius.
ALBURT EYENSTINE CAMOOSE.

"Make mine a treble".   P.P.A.HOLE.
(How did he get in the credits? the man's a menace. A. Note.)

STOP THE PRESS! STOP THE PRESS! STOP THE PRESS!

With the arrival of Spring 2003, I've had a creative upsurge, creating four new pieces and setting up a writer's evening at Platform One Art Gallery in Todmorden, for April 16th (it would have been my mother's 79th birthday if she'd been alive, and not dead since 1986; how could she do this to me? Not be there for my moment of glory [it didn't last for much more than a moment] the selfish old lady); the first 2 pieces are included in 'DEEPER THAN NOTHINGNESS', already at the printer's; 'DOWN IN ONE' is already published, that just leaves 'COPING WITH MADNESS' to correct and complete, adding these two latest literary gems.

....

SPRING FEVER, (I'VE JUST CAUGHT A NASTY COLD I KNOW THAT.) 2/4/03.

I've got it! I'm like a randy old tomcat on heat, albeit a bit neutered. I'm feeling fidgety and restless, and looking furtively at young women's arses; I saw a few top shags while I was out today. But no one else seems to be suffering from this strange reproductive malaise, not a hint, not a flicker of sexual abandon have I detected, everyone but me seems perfectly normal.
Perhaps everyone else in Calderdale, even the o.a.p's, is sorted out for sexual satisfaction; everyone except 'use 'em and lose em', 'hump 'em and dump 'em' (in my mind anyway) ME! And even my plans of escaping to Thailand for my annual fuck are in jeopardy with this new strain of Asian killer flu'; tourists are being advised now by the foreign office not to travel to Hong Kong or Southern China, and Thailand's the next stop! Trying to get your end away in this country, if you're not an instantly desirable proposition, is filled with more potential traps and pitfalls than an 18-page, DSS, 'INCAPACITY FOR WORK' form, and you're so stressed out after filling one of those in, you need a shag to de-stress yourself; in my case this wasn't forthcoming.
At the respectable end of the sex market, (tho' there's no shortage of sharks in these 'lonely parts' infested waters, not least the shysters who charge £1-£1.50p a minute for this 'service'), are the WLTM columns, acres of lonely love bunnies

looking for Mr Big Knob, with loads of cash to spend on them, the sad twats. 'Possible relationship' is dangled at the end of every ad', so if you're daft enough you can spend a small fortune merely trying to locate, and pin down to a date, one of these thinking man's shrinking violets. And if she does turn up, her rat-like brain will be working overtime, "Is he a total minger or what? How quickly can I ditch him? After dessert, a liqueur and an 'After Eight'? Don't want my mates to see what I've been out with, oh God, what have I done!?" And you're definitely not the fathering of her babies material. "Well, thanks for the meal, I don't think we're compatible, you'll meet someone, someday." Bah! So you've forked out 40 or 50 quid, made an effort to look the part, and you end up feeling more complexed than if you'd not bothered with all this rigmarole in the first place. I think 'speed dating's' got a lot going for it, three minutes for both parties to make their minds up, fucking brilliant! That's about as long as the average shag can last if you're lucky anyway.

I've no objection to paying for sex if I'm going to be treated with some respect, I'm not a piece of meat, and neither is my penis. Street tarts are usually the 'scrag end' of the sex trade; you've got to be really desperate to stoop that low; tho' I wouldn't say no to an 18-year-old (just inside the law), unless she was too run down thru' 'crack' and 'smack' abuse, (and we're not talking spanking abuse here). Escorts cost more, but that wouldn't bother me, our Yorkshire version of 'METRO', the free newspaper, was allowing escorts to advertise in the specially created Adults section towards the end of last year. One lady advertised herself as 'Edina of Wetherby', a high-class hooker by the sound of her, and there were escort agencies as well. I kept telling myself to write the phone number down of a Leeds-based one, because I knew that the insidious forces of 'moral concern' were going to stick their festering beaks in and get this harmless little section closed down; but another voice said, "What's the point? They'll be out of my price range, and Leeds is a long way off", and sure enough, it was closed down and replaced with an ad' for a 'gay' chat line, at least that's gone as well now, the dirty arse-shagging bastards! (This is my own opinion, I know I could be had up for homophobic sentiments, but no amount of legislation will convince me that homosexuality is not a perversion of sexuality; they're wired up the wrong way; and rather than celebrating this abnormal trait in both sexes, [and I also think that lesbians are more dangerous and corrupt than male homosexuals], medical science should concentrate on finding a cure for it; I suppose I'll now be on a hit list of the militant lesbian brigade, who won't be happy until they see me publicly castrated...with a blunt razor blade. 4/7/06.) (At this time of correcting this proof, 1/5.03, it's been re-instated.)

All of which still leaves me holding my prick in my hand, to take me to the promised land of orgasm for one.

....

A SEXY VOICE ON RADIO, AND ME.
2/4/03.

There's an affinity between a sexy voice on the radio and me, though she doesn't know it. With me it's bordering on fixation, the 'saddo's' ultimate sin of projecting their lonely and unrequited urges onto a friendly person. In this instance, she's a presenter on a late night radio station, Friday and Saturday nights, early in the A.M; not as forlorn as the actual 'graveyard shift' of 4 to 7am. She's been on the radio for years, mainly at the weekends, 6 hours a week. I wonder what she does with the other 162 hours in any given week? I would like to write and ask her, but having recently written to her for a photo to go with the voice, I'm afraid she might start thinking I'm harassing or stalking her; I've figured on sending her an Xmas card with a photo of my erect penis enclosed, (taken in a passport foto booth; it heightens the risk-taking buzz one gets in exposing one's self), and not saying who it's from.
I'd love it if a member of the opposite sex sent me a photo of her fanny ('cunt' for the American market), close up with her legs open, exposing loads of inner thigh, preferably fingering herself; I

don't know if this precarious and perilous position could be achieved on a passport foto booth stool, alas I probably never will.
She has sent me a photo of her lovely face, she's got 'come to heaven' eyes, I wonder what her inner thighs are like? I think she's a Christian, so she wouldn't take kindly to be asked such a question from me; I'd love to lick her out. (drinking from the furry loving cup); I really don't know what's brought this mood of coarseness on. Maybe she's psychically transmitting repressed sexual urges to me, or maybe it's a sex vampire looking for any excuse to 'milk' me of my vital fluids? It will be disappointed if it is, because most of my semen is going back down again as a side effect of some prostate gland medication I'm taking in an effort to shrink it. When I've finished this course of treatment, (I've had some mixed results from it, virtually spunkless wanks being one of them), I'm going to try pollen extract; at least I know now that the burning sensation and poor urine flow I've suffered with for the last 20 years or so isn't necessarily wholly due to an STD. It could just as well be due to 'prostatitis' or 'prostatodynia', which are difficult to diagnose and treat.
It's strange to have a woman's face staring at me from on top of my gas fire, next to my Vincent Van Gogh post cards, (sent by him to the, as then, unborn me, sympathising with my lonely plight [from the loony bin at Arles], stuck in every night writing shite like this; tho' I've left copyright of all

my work to WSPA, so that any posthumous
royalties that may accrue will go to saving
endangered animal species, unlike you Vincent, [I
write to him on the Astral Plain you know],
who've been ripped off mercilessly by the very
system you hated most, the art market)
Yes, her smiling bemusedly at me, gives me a little
thrill, makes me feel less completely alone in this
man-made hell on Earth; I think I'll write and
thank her for her trouble, but no, it's something
they all do, radio DJs, they may even have a
budget for it. I think I'll stick to the Xmas card
idea without the rude pic' of my own private part
whose warmth occasionally thaws out my frozen
heart…I might just start
fantasising about her when she's in bed with me
(on the radio) at the weekends.

....

(PLF. Well that's definitely it! Once this collection
has been put into book form, it will complete my
quartet; I hope they're all more accessible than
that old fogey T.S. Eliot's 'Four Quartets'
are/were, let alone his 'WASTELAND'; if it was
left to me they'd be let alone forever; the foggy,
highbrow twaddle. But who am I to cast
aspersions on someone else's work? Who am I?
Won't somebody tell me? More to the point, WHY

AM I??? I seem to serve no other function than to produce these accounts of social exclusion and isolation; I think I deserve better.)
8/4/03.)

(PLF. May Day, 2003. Anti Capitalist riot day, the new tradition; why can't these moronic hippies stay in their communes and squats, and leave the rest of us to our consumer frenzy? It's good to spend cash, and it keeps third world people in jobs, there's no state benefit for them.
I wrote somewhere recently, that I'm sick of writing parables for the lost and the lonely, so hopefully I won't be doing it anymore. When I write now, I want it to be cool and laid back, and preferably funny too. Whether this gets into print will be dependent on whether I get back safely from Thailand or not; I go on this coming Sunday. Actually, just as a final footnote, this should have been my third collection, not my fourth, but who gives a fuck! Not me, that's for sure. [What a terrible 'old hippy' attitude to have for a crypto fascist like me. Oh no! Now no-one will buy my work if they see the 'f' word.])

....

As part of my fetish for 'burying' new work just in case I get famous and the anoraks who like nothing better than scouring other people's efforts with a fine tooth comb, should eventually locate this, the final new edition to 'my family' of modern poetic creations; I genuinely do try to avoid writing any more work that's going to be ignored in an ever more frenetic climate of fear and loathing in the modern world.

A lot of people are just far too busy to sit around reading 'door stopper' thick books, which seems to make authors more determined to keep producing them. The sum total of my eight collections (nine if you include my blog) only amounts to about 500 pages; our more prolific writers produce a 5 to 600-page manuscript every year or so, take Stephen King as an example.

Incidentally, this piece hasn't even appeared on my blog, it's entirely new, I only created it this morning (29/9/07), tho' some of the ideas have been floating in my brain for a few days; I'll be staring it on a fresh computer page.

STRANGLEHOLD.   29/9/07.

The difference between sexual biology and psychology is sensitivity,
And an over sensitive male does not make the ladies hot;
Recreational sex is the best outlet for relieving stress that we've
Got. I only ever hit the G-spot once in my prime, and now that I've

Got lots of time to think about sex there's a hex on my libido.

I'm lying in bed listening to music literally inside my head,
Courtesy of my faithful old personal stereo radio cassette player's
Earphones. I feel sorry for people who've never discovered the
Delights of radio, other than Radio 1, the 'yoof station to which
My listening days have long since gone, tho' I'm still partial
To a bit of Judge Jules and Pete Tong.

Before 'House' and 'Dance' music came along, my interest in
Pop music had virtually gone; I was stuck in a time warp
Around Al Stewart's 'YEAR OF THE CAT', music took on
A much harsher tone after that with the advent of 'punk',
With much worse still to come, the 'thrash' and 'death' metal
Scum for instance, as well as the 'new romantics.'

Generationally speaking, I'm far too old to supposedly enjoy
Dance music, I'd look like a really sad old git if I tried 'larging it'

In Ibiza or Falaraki, but this new psychedelic sound with its
Pumping, thumping rhythms, really does it for me; and I envy
The carefree young who can party all night long and get away
With it.

I think euthanasia should be a routine tool in the fight against
Senility; once you've become incontinent and insane you should
Be put out of your misery humanely, not kept 'alive' because
Society doesn't want to be seen as harsh or judgemental; pity
The poor carer of an advanced case of Alzheimer's disease say I,
I'm sure at times they want to die as much as the actual sufferer.

It should be the quality and not the quantity of human life that counts,
But we're living in an age where extremism rather enlightenment
Dominates; the politics of fear and hate are driven by a determined few.
Oppressive regimes could be removed by a million pairs of
Angry feet on the street chanting, 'PEOPLE POWER, PEOPLE POWER!

Military dictatorships can't hold out against a sheer weight
Of numbers, this is a historical fact.

Aged 60, I'm now concentrating on my own personal paradise;
My version of the afterlife might differ greatly from yours.
It'll be just me, aged 23, and a whole harem of beautiful women
Living miles apart in an idyllic green and lush setting, letting me
Play Lord and Master whenever I deigned to pay them a visit,
(this is the afterlife we're talking about here ladies, though if
you've read these sentiments I'm sure there will be some of you who'd
love to string me up so I could get there quicker.)
There'll be no mechanical noise of any kind, only magical colours
And the best music I can find in my youthful eternity.

....

And that's it, please let that be it; if I ever get the urge to write again you can shoot me and speed me on my way to my happy everafter, where the sounds of sex and laughter are all I'll hear.

www.ingramcontent.com/pod-product-compliance
Lightning Source LLC
Chambersburg PA
CBHW051759040426
42446CB00007B/446